The Satanic Bible

By

Rev. Caesar 999

Copyright © 1999 All Rights Reserved
Rev. Caesar 999

ISBN 13: 978-0-615-16991-0

Table of Contents

Introduction 5
Part I The Orders 14
Part II The Principles 20
Part III Regulations 31
Part IV Goals 50
Part V Rituals and Ceremonies 64
Part VI Satanic Evolution 68
Part VII The Eye of Satan 101
Part VIII Satan's Hammer 212
Part IX Holy Days 218
Part X The Great House of Polygamy 220
Part XI Advanced Principles 225
Part XII The New Sciences 231
Part XIII Temple of Kama 236
Part XIV The Nine Satanic Statements 242
Part XV The Anti-Saints 246

Introduction

Part 1-A LaVeyian Satanism
And
Authoritarianism

We are through playing games. If you haven't figured out my sincerity yet, then you never will. The time has come for us to examine my beliefs more closely. I'm going to break them down as simply as I can, for the benefit of the intellect and the nonintellect. To understand my beliefs, we must first understand the basics of most other popularized forms of Satanism.

Let us begin with LaVey's and companies Philosophy. Most of the COS splinter groups follow the same basic philosophy, except for minor organizational differences. They believe in what I call Puritan Individualism, which is total Self-Godhood. This means absolutely nothing comes before them, except maybe family and loved ones. There is no core loyalty or benefit of the whole. This is why I call it a mercenary belief system.

They also combine a bit of objectivism into their beliefs, where they believe that they are not victims or that they are not oppressed in anyway. This in a sense denies the reality of forces beyond your control, which have ultimately affected a greater percentage of the outcome of your achievements in your lifetime. I don't believe in all of the concepts of objectivism. LaVeyian philosophy is against all organized religion, which reveals their own business like hypocrisy. This cult of atheists has no real religious message or higher goals to attain. They therefore, stand against the simplest idealism, the same idealism that has raised society up out of the depths of human chaos and misguided confusion, and Laveyians are without any real goals to rise up and achieve! Though, Laveyian Satanists do accept the need to embrace those fantasy ideals in their rituals as long

as they do not ultimately sink into a nonsensical belief that denies the carnal fulfillment of Man and Woman.
Through fantasy we fulfill a psychological need. This I agree with, but why confine those ideals to our rituals alone? If Satanism is fulfillment, then why not indulge in the pleasures of our Idealistic Fantasies on a full-time basis?
Maybe the ancients, who were not nonsensical, did this very thing. To me fantasy and reality are very close and sometimes one can not be determined from the other. If something can not be proved or disproved, it is a fantasy, but it can never be denied from reality completely.

Part 1-B Laveyian Satanism And Authoritarianism

So, believing in such fantasy beliefs can do no harm directly as long as we realize that they are never an absolute truth, but merely our personal truths! Therefore, no group, order, or religion, has the right to enforce all of their beliefs, moral-values, etc., upon other people, groups, etc. This would infringe upon the Natural Spiritual Rights of others, which again laveyian objectivism opposes and means they believe that there are no natural rights at all. This includes primeval rights as opposed to Spiritual Rights, the only thing I do agree with.
As primeval creatures, we had no rights, but we have evolved, through our spiritual ideals, creating society and higher civilization, based upon natural foundational spiritual rights. Many groups, religions go beyond the foundational basics and create laws to enforce all of their moralvalues, even upon people of opposing moral-values which harm no others. cHristianity totally enforces their moral-values, beliefs, etc., upon others through civil laws, that oppresses billions and creates a nonsensical belief system, which goes against human nature and our carnal fulfillment, as would any other belief system that rises to such fanaticism.
So, Laveyian Satanists can not argue about judeo-christianities nonsensical beliefs, which makes them sound like a victim to me, through their belief that there are no true natural rights. The purpose of society is to secure humanities Spiritual Rights and raise us from the jungle. Though some where humanity took a wrong turn down the road of nonsensical religion. They also didn't fully realize the science that I'm now revealing to you, which only effects living beings and will eternally transcend

our idealistic spiritual beliefs, polluting our Spiritual Society with the Natural Scientific Laws of Dominion!
They are scientific because they can be proven beyond a shadow of a doubt. This means they are purely realistic/materialistic, not spiritual or fantasy bound. These laws need to be incorporated into the very foundations of the schools of society and used to benefit our society.
These laws are and have always been incorporated into the natural world and our societies, but I doubt that they were always taught and used in the erecting of society. These 4 principles reveal the authoritarian nature of animal society. These are the principles we all use, most unknowingly and will always affect our lives. These are the Natural Authoritarian Laws that all organizations use to dominate their enemies. These are the laws christianity uses to oppress us, through their moral-value system transformed into civil laws. Therefore, I'm not against these true natural laws. This means I believe in fighting fire with fire. We will defeat judeo-christianity through Counter-Authoritarianism! This does not mean we will force them to believe in our principles, it just means we will take back our Spiritual (Religious) Rights through the true Laws of Nature! This is what I mean by saying that Satanism must become a real religion and not some false religion, an anti-religion.

1. Dominate or be Dominated.
2. Strength in Numbers.
3. New and Better Knowledge always prevails over Old and Useless Knowledge.
4. Order controls Chaos.

Part 2 Traditional Satanism
And
The Philosophy of 999

There have been many so-called Satanic groups over the years, but very few were actually Satanic in the christian sense, but were of course deemed so through christian beliefs. Most of these groups and religions were in existence before christianity or sprung up around the same time as the foundation of christianity and were undoubtedly rivals for power and control. Christianity, made it very clear that they were the dominant authoritarian power through its whole extermination and destruction of peoples, cultures, religions, and their histories. Some of these Groups and Religions were the Cathars, Luciferians, Waldensians, and even the Knights Templars who combined Mithraism with christianity, etc.

Later on, there were other groups like the english Hell-Fire Club and then Dashwood's Hell-Fire Club. The motto of the club was borrowed from Rabelais, "Fay Ce Que Voudras!" This means, Do What You Will! This is very similar to Crowley's Motto, "There Is No Grace, There Is No Guilt. This Is The Law, Do What Thou Wilt!" I think Crowley borrowed it as well!

The term Traditional Satanist, has come to mean a Satanist that believes in more Traditional Satanic Philosophies, Religions, etc. The main aspect of these so-called Traditional beliefs is a belief in and worshipping of the actual christian devil and the evil that it represents.

In my opinion, there are very few if any Truly Traditional Groups in existence and therefore these Satanists and Traditional Satanic Groups are actually contemporary or modern groups, a name which Lavey has popularized for His own adopted beliefs.

In reality, all of these groups and different denominations are truly representative of Contemporary Satanic Groups and Beliefs, including all of these foolish pagan groups as well! My Philosophy of The 999 brings us to my beliefs, which ultimately combine aspects of all these Contemporary Satanic Beliefs. This means it's a combination of so-called Contemporary Satanism and so-called Traditional Satanism! My Satan is the Deity and Divinity of Creation. We are a part of Creation and therefore, we are the Lesser Deities/Divinities of Creation. Within all of Creation, the duality exists and also the dueling of Creation. This Creation has a Dark Force and a Light Force, a Masculine Force, and a Feminine Force, a Positive Force, and a Negative Force. As a product of Creation, we are a reflection of this Androgynous Creation and therefore we are Androgynous Beings, Naturally Bisexual and physically separated as Man and Woman, the Duality of Creation.

I believe that the number nine represents not only the end of a cycle, but the beginning as well. This is the Greek Alpha and the Omega!

This is symbolic of Completion and represents the eternal cycle of life and death and of Creation itself. Therefore, it is a sacred number of Creation and Spirituality/Religion. I use three nines to symbolically represent My Holy Trinity of Satan.

The nine in the center represents Androgynous Creation, our God/Goddess and the New Completed Religion. It is completed because after each resurrection of society from the ashes of imperfection and uselessness, it is finally rising in a state of perfection, The Golden Phoenix!!! The nine to the right represents Man and His Conservatism. The nine to the left represents Woman and Her Liberalism. Together they fulfill the Divine Marriage and represent a state of Balance and Resurrection Achieved!!! This is My Mysticism, My Reality and Fantasy! This is My Androgynous Creation, My Bisexual God/Goddess! This is My Satan, My-Self!

Part 3 Vampir Satanism 999
And
Satan's Vampir Knights

The whole concept of Vampir Satanism begins with the belief that Life or Creation is Vampiric in nature, from the beginning. This is the concept of Life feeding on Life to survive! Therefore, we are all born Vampir and don't truly require the assistance of another Vampir to become a Vampir. Though, this is done very symbolically and is representative of Sacred Initiation!

Blood is a Divinely Sacred Symbol in the world of Vampirism, representing the source and Power of all Life, Immortal Life! Vampirism may stand on its own as a religion, just like Satanism may stand on its own as a way of Life. Though, I feel that Vampirism becomes a true religion when combined with the principles of a true religion.

Therefore, Vampirism combined with my Satanism 999, becomes Vampir Satanism 999 as recognized through my Satanic Vampir Creed! There is also the aspect of the Sorcerer and the Warrior that is combined here. Since, the original meaning of a Vampir was a type of Sorcerer and we can say that their Power is attained through their Blood and others Blood. This is like kundalini, chi, tao, or the dao, etc.

This is also the same as the force in star wars and is the Power of The Martial Artist. This Power must be perfected through Purification. The Blood must be Pure! This leads to the Art of Alchemy and the foundation of The Martial Temple of Satanic Vampir Knights!!!

This Priestly Order has Four Degrees of Mastery:
1. The Vampir/ess, The Initiate.
2. Priest/ess, The First Degree of Mastery.
3. Priest/ess, The Second Degree of Mastery.
4. Androgynist, The Ultimate Degree of Mastery.

Part I The Orders

Satan's Vampir Knights

Purpose and Goal

Welcome Satanic Vampires! I am an Ordained Priest and the sole founder of this infant order. I like to call myself The First Priest, instead of High Priest. I hope you've enjoyed some of my esoteric spiritual scriptures. If you didn't, maybe this path isn't for you. I don't expect you to take them all literally, just with a sense of spiritual awareness. Yes, this is a path of spirituality, as well as materialism. Like many, I believe in a balance and maintaining that balance. To me, the essence and heart of the mind, is the soul. This is my balance, the spiritual and material, mental and physical. I consider myself a Warrior-Priest. Therefore, this is the path of the Spiritual Warrior, The Martial Way. I have decided on using a simple military ranking system. This system corresponds to my ideals and appeals to my sense of order and sophistication. Everyone starts out weak and will grow stronger or die. Out of this process, we have visualized and made our path. This was and always shall be the ultimate goal, improvement of the self. If during this process, we happen to change the world, then so be it!

Training

If you decide to join my temple, your training will begin immediately. You will be tested for your physical health and strength. In addition, you will also be tested for your intelligence and knowledge. Therefore, your training will consist of two branches, the mental/spiritual and the physical/material. As the guardians of the temple, we will be prepared mentally and physically, to stave off attack, from our enemies!

Mental/Spiritual

Your knowledge of religion and spirituality, will help to mold and perfect your greater personality and spiritual awareness. Your personality and spiritual awareness in turn effects your physical health and vice versa. This is where your knowledge of spiritual healing, will benefit you and others. This knowledge will transcend to actual physical healing. All of this is necessary, for you are to be a Warrior-Priest or Warrior-Priestess. Eventually, we hope to reach out to other branches of knowledge, to offer an alternative mental path.

Physical/Material

Your physical training will help maintain your physical health and again, vice versa. Remember that the body is our temple! We must purify the temple with clean water and fresh air. So, we try to eliminate poisons and toxins from our bodies and from entering our bodies in the first place. We do this because these poisons and toxins will contaminate us and cause mental and physical illness. Therefore, we will combine the use of proper nutrition and regimented exercise, to maintain maximum health. This will be achieved through the development of our spiritual health consciousness.

Rank and File

Rank is something very sacred that must be earned righteously and honorably! As your progress grows, you will be tested, along the way.
If you pass your tests, you will be granted the proper Rank and privileges. I expect you, to do your best, climbing The Mountain of Glory!

Satan's Vampir Healers

This is The Order of The Sacred Sexual/Spiritual Healers! This Order is made up of three classes of Healers. Each class is separated by the degree or level of healing that they perform. Whether or not they charge a fee for their services is their personal and sacred right and no one will take this sacred right away from them without facing the Knights and Soldiers of this Church Of The Antichrist. These Sacred Priests and Priestesses are the Holy Whores of Babylon or the Divine Prostitutes that support the foundation of Our New World Economy. Through their Sacred Work, we shall fill the Golden Vaults of Babylon once again and raise Our Holy Order from judeo-christian oppression to the Final and Glorious Seats of Judgement. Hail The Holy Whore! Hail The Sacred Prostitute! Hail the Church Of The Antichrist!

Satan's Vampir Army

This military institution is the main body and vanguard of our movement. This organization is a separate entity, from Satan's Vampir Knight's Of The Temple! The Knights are an elite order, The Priestess/Priesthood, devoted to serving and protecting Satan's Divine Vampir Temple! Though, everyone who joins the Church Of The Antichrist, is automatically considered a Warrior-Priest/Priestess, a royally devout soldier of The Ideal Antichrist! Our Militia is an order dedicated to protecting The Satanic Vampir People! Therefore, this is The People's Satanic Vampir Army! This citizens' militia and the Knights are sworn to live by and uphold the values of Satan's Divine Vampir Bible and The Satanic Vampir Creed! Beyond those values, there will be very few mandates for the militia, unlike those that the Knights must adhere to. One of your other jobs as a soldier will be to recruit new members into our organization. You will be given a monetary commission for each new member that you bring into our organization. Therefore, this is one way that you can benefit by being a member of our organization. If you become an agent for us today, tomorrow you will definitely profit!

Part II The Principles

The Virtuous Principles
_Of_
Satanism 999

1. *Allegiance*
2. *Brotherhood/Sisterhood*
3. *Truth/Respect*
4. *New World Order*
5. *Sexual Freedom*
6. *Life*

1. **Allegiance** *represents duty and becomes, "The Grand Responsibility of The True Nobility!"*
2. **Brotherhood and Sisterhood** *represents love and strength, which becomes, "The Apocalyptic Embracement of Hatred!"*
3. **Truth and Respect** *represents honor and integrity, becoming, "The Sacred Acceptance!"*
4. **New World Order** *represents new world religion, rebirth, youth, and beauty, becoming, "The Divine Resurrection!"*
5. **Sexual Freedom** *represents release, relief, and fulfillment, becoming, "The Realization and Spiritual Enlightenment of The Holy Union!"*
6. **Life** *represents triumph and immortality, which is, "The Providential Existence!"*

Prologue Part 1 The Solution

I do not have to receive an orthodox education, to be an intelligent, knowledgeable, Priest and Healer! I especially, do not have to be a clean-cut conformist, dressed in a monkey-suit, to be a professional! I am a mystic Warrior-Priest! I call my belief system Vampir Satanism 999, The Antichrist Solution! Through my religion, I offer social, economic, and religious salvation, to my Satanic Brothers and Sisters! Nine Nine Nine, is Satan's Divine Trinity! Nine is the end of a cycle and the end symbolizes the beginning. Therefore, Nine is a divine number, representing the beginning and the end, the alpha and the omega! This is the number of my androgynous Goddess/God! Men and Women are one with creation and so we are our own individual lesser Goddesses and Gods! This means Nine is also the number of Woman and Man! Through the Divine Marriage, we become one and so three Nines represent our oneness! The middle Nine represents, our Goddess/God and the New Religion! The Nine to the right represents, Man and his Conservatism! The Nine to the left represents, Woman and her Liberalism! Together, the three Nines represent Balance and Resurrection!

Prologue Part 2 The Sign

I have chosen this hexagram as my personal seal! This hexagram is a symbol that represents the greater consciousness of creation, in the macrocosm and the lesser consciousness of the human psyche, in the microcosm! Therefore, this symbol of creation represents my great androgynous Goddess/God and the lesser Goddess/Gods, Men and Women! Since we are a part of creation, we realize our oneness, with creation itself! This is the Divine Union or Divine Marriage, between Brother and Sister, and our androgynous Goddess/God! I have tattooed this talismanic symbol of creation upon my forehead, so that others can see it and bare witness, as it is a sign of initiation into a New Religious Order! Through initiation, it becomes a symbol of devotion, which means sacrifice! I am founding this Order as its first initiate, self-baptized, as The Avenger, The First Priest of Satan's Divine Vampir Temple! I now reveal to the world, my New Moral-Value System! Behold, "Satan's Divine Vampir Bible!" This is our true book of revelation, free and devoid of foundational hypocrisy, institutional dogma, and unwarranted bias! I am The Apostle of Satan and the time is now!

Prologue Part 3 My Fantasy

What I believe is my fantasy! There is no truth here, but my truth! My real God is Myself! No one can say to me that is dogma! Everyone is a hypocrite, especially me! If you say, I'm not a hypocrite then you are a lying hypocrite! This book contains my Moral-Value System! No one can say this system or that system is the right system, that is institutionalized dogma! This system is for those who believe in it! My goal is to dethrone, the judeo-christian Moral-Value System! No system should have authority over the whole! If it does, then you have been subjugated by that very religion, its leaders, and the believers or followers of that religion! This means church and state/federal authority is only partially severed on a legal level and not at all, on an ethical level! If we are going to have separation, we must have a true, total, and complete separation of church and state/federal authority! Otherwise, each state must have the power to authorize and dictate its own ethical standards and policies!

Let me introduce you to, The Satanic State! This will be the state, within the state, the power, within the power! Through my state authority, we shall completely overthrow, the judeo-christian Moral-Value System! Hail Satan!

The Moral of Allegiance

Everyone who believes in their society is responsible for their society, just as much as it is responsible for you, because your society exists to serve you, the loyal people! This means your society must provide all physical and psychological needs that are essential to your continuing health. Therefore, you will prove your true allegiance, through your duty, the work you must do. If your society cannot provide everyone with work, then those governing your society are at fault, not the people, because of lack of employment. If you are proven unhealthy and incapable of working, you will be granted impunity. If there is opportunity for employment and you are perfectly capable of working and you still choose not to work, then you are guilty of disloyalty, nonallegiance! For this crime, these people will be deported from the state or penalized into a work force program, to attain maximum efficiency. Allegiance is the heart of all great societies and when it is completely lost, so is the society. Ultimately, "The Grand Responsibility of The True Nobility," is the duty each of us must perform, revealing the depths of our great allegiance. Allegiance is the moral glue, holding together our sacred Brotherhood and Sisterhood. We must cherish our moral of allegiance, for it is the life blood and foundation, raising up our social temple, The New Satanic State!

**The Moral of Brotherhood
And
Sisterhood**

From time to time, the people of the world have captured the true essence of the family structure. Our great family structure includes aspects of idealistic/spiritualistic and materialistic/realistic codes that make it a solid, worthy structure. This means there are no cracks, weak spots, or holes, no Achilles heel that can be penetrated, by enemies of the state. Allegiance is the bloodline of the Brotherhood and Sisterhood, which reveals our true love, giving our family structure its strength, rising to defeat all opposition in the final earth war, "The Apocalyptic Embracement of Hatred!" Everyone must embrace their hate, accepting it, understanding who and why you are! Through this, you'll know what you believe in and for whom do you stand? Do you stand for or against, The Apostle of Satan? I say, love your loyal Brothers and Sisters, and hate disloyalty!

The Moral of Truth and Respect

Truth and Respect work side by side. Without Truth, there is no Respect and vice versa! If there is no Truth or Respect, there is no Love, no Allegiance, and no Brotherhood or Sisterhood! Through our moral of Truth and Respect, we gain personal and public honor and integrity. All of us seek acceptance in one form or another, becoming a psychological and physical goal as with all The Satanic Morals. This ultimately leads us to "The Sacred Acceptance!" The Sacred Acceptance is learning to accept people of all race and sexuality into The New State. However, this excludes people promoting and supporting all religions representing the judeo-christian Moral-Value System! These religions are hypocritical, biased, and dogmatized, claiming that their principles are the only moral truth, yet it is only their truth! Through this claim, people with different moral principles are mocked, degraded, and made outcasts of free society???
The peoples' government adopted its formal system of ethics from a dominating religious majority. This was a christian majority, enforcing its rule, even though church and state authority, had supposedly been severed, long ago??? What this means, is that we are still ruled by, christian authoritarianism, through religious/political intervention! This in turn outcasts even more people because of authoritarian laws made according to those adopted ethics. These laws should not exist and shall cease to exist in "The New Satanic State!"
"We shall break the whip of oppression, swallowing the lords of christian society and the tumultuous masses of right-wing masochists, spreading, The Satanic Temple, to the four corners of the earth!!!"

The Moral of A New World Order

All of us, seek youth and beauty, the symbols of perfection. So the old becomes a symbol of uselessness and imperfection, driving us toward new and better creations. Through our longing for these new and better creations, we arrive at a great spiritual rebirth, through a New World Religion. This new world religion timelessly erects a New World Order through "The Divine Resurrection!" For the old isn't truly destroyed, only reborn, and redesigned, better than before, insuring us with new hope, new faith, and new allegiance! All of these beliefs and ideals help bring us toward the acceptance of The New Phoenix rising from its ashes of uselessness and imperfection! Behold The Perfected One, Resurrected, bringing forth the principles of The New World Religion, Vampir Satanism 999!!!

The Moral of Sexual Freedom

Sexual freedom means just that, the freedom of any willing adult to engage in sexual relations with any other willing adult without discrimination or condemnation. This is the absolute acceptance of a person's sexuality, be it heterosexual, homosexual, or bisexual, etc. This person's sexuality also includes whether or not they are abstinent or promiscuous, polygamous or monogamous, permanently cohabiting, or even a soliciting prostitute! We shall never accept moral judgment, based upon sexual behavior, only true character! The release of our sexual anxieties brings us relief and fulfillment of our sexual desires. Through this we are freed of possible deeper more complex psychological disorders caused by sexual repression. Our moral of Truth and Respect guides us with "The Sacred Acceptance!" of all anti-christian people toward "The Realization and Spiritual Enlightenment of The Holy Union!" The Holy Union is The Divine Marriage between ourselves in our Brotherhood and Sisterhood to our androgynous Goddess/God of creation. For we are all one!
"Then when the Goddess/God finally awoke from its sleep, mortality was just a dream, slowly forgotten!"
"**Satan** is the father of truth and the mother of desire. Lies are only beliefs until they are proven false and the will, only control, until dethronement by a superior power. For christianity, will be overthrown by, The Masters' of The Black Arts!"
"**Homosexuality** breaks through the veils of pseudo-christian purity and frees the androgynous nature of Man and Woman. For the true God is unmasked in the souls of Men and Women, through the freedom of expression, especially, sexual expression!" **Satan's Sorcery-Volume I**

The Moral of Life

Life is a magnificently divine phenomenon, echoing through an eternal saga, climaxing out of our flight from Death in the ultimate triumph, Immortality! From our Sacred Marriage to the Goddess/God we are spiritually enlightened to our own God and Goddesshood. Through this we realize our potential for escaping Death becoming literal Gods and Goddesses. This motivational potential is the divine fuel or divine power that will finally escalate humanity into "The Providential Existence!" The Phoenix rises, dressed anew, with golden feathers as we bless Her for our cosmic voyage. She is purified, baptized through fire. This is an initiation and the inauguration of a New Golden Age! Fly with me, loyal Brothers and Sisters. Fly with me, to the heavens!!! I am your Avenger, The Apostle of Satan!!!

"If you want disciples, follow yourself! If you want lovers, love yourself! If you want truth, believe in yourself! If you want Life, Live!!!" **Satan's Sorcery Volume II**

Part III Regulations

Antichrist Blacklist

1. Boy Scouts of America
We are hereby blacklisting the "Boy Scouts of America" and all other organizations, which associate and support them and their beliefs! They are a christian organization, which has publicly denounced and condemned the beautiful, legitimate, and growing lifestyle of homosexuality!
2. Roman Catholic Church
We are hereby blacklisting the "Roman Catholic Church" and all its protestant fissures! The church has stood as a blockade to true moral freedom, for far too many centuries. They have killed millions in the name of god and christ. They have outcast the innocent and destroyed truly advanced knowledge. They have stood as a front for organized crime and acted as true blood sucking vampires, draining their own people of their precious and hard earned wealth. Therefore, they have grown fat and arrogant in the name of god, while three quarters of the people of the world still live in absolute destitute. The people of the world have been forced into a totally preventable calamity, known as poverty, by their very own religious/political leaders. You might think after two thousand years, if they were altruistic or divine, that poverty would not exist, gays and prostitutes would be respected and loved for their true character, that they would not egotistically claim to possess the only true god and the only true moral-value system. The roman catholic church will be leveled to the ground by my sword of truth, my new moral-value system!
3. U.S. Military
We are hereby blacklisting all branches of the "U.S. Military!" They have come a long way when it comes to equal rights for women, but their hypocritically shifty attitude toward homosexuality has deemed them unworthy and unsupportive

proponents of gay rights, thereby warranting blacklist status! They obviously are representing and supporting right-wing christian moral-values! A point to military command. We want you to remember The Greek Army, because they conquered most of the world! Fear The Gay Army! NO GUTS, NO GLORY!!!

Birth-Rights or The Right To Life

1. The Right to Live Free in your own personal environment!
2. The Right to Fulfill All of your Reasonable Desires and Needs!
3. The Right to Destroy your Oppressor!
4. The Right to Attain Possessions!
5. The Right to Believe what You Will!

You're only a servant, never a slave, until you say and believe that you have no rights! You have the rights to live free and to fulfill your reasonable desires! If you are not free and cannot legally fulfill your reasonable desires, you have become an oppressed servant of the ruling power! In reality, you are a slave to the dominant force, though spiritually you'll never be a real slave if you believe in your personal rights as a living being! You have The Birth-Rights or The Rights To Life, so don't ever let anyone tell you, that you have no rights! For at that moment, you'll become a slave to the higher ruling power and to those who deceive you by telling you such lies and nonsense!

Sacred Regulations
Of
Satan's Vampir Knights

1. All Warrior-Priest/ess must complete the Secret Regulation!
2. All Warrior-Priest/ess must keep their heads shaven as a sign of initiation and sacrifice!
3. All Warrior-Priest/ess must not use drugs or alcohol, only sparingly during sacred ritual upon the Greater or Lesser Sabbath, The Great Saturnalia, Saturday, and other selected holy days!
4. All Warrior-Priest/ess must join one more creditable Satanic, Vampir, or Thelemaic organization!
5. All Warrior-Priest/ess must study religion, magick, and the occult in general!
6. All Warrior-Priest/ess must train in at least one form of martial art!
7. All Warrior-Priest/ess must eat healthy nutritious diets, including regular and regimented daily exercise!
8. All Warrior-Priest/ess must have a healthy amount of deep sleep and REM sleep each day!

Satan's Vampir Knights

Basic Rules of Ministry

1. Satan's Ministers will obey all commands of The Supreme Master, The High Priest and General of The Legion or face expulsion; excommunication! For Satanism 999, represents absolute Allegiance!
2. Satan's Ministers will not preach against, mock, or defame other Ministers of Satan's Divine Vampir Temple! For Satanism 999, represents true Brotherhood and Sisterhood!
3. Satan's Ministers will not lie to their Disciples! For Satanism 999, represents Truth and Respect!
4. Satan's Ministers will not support judeo-christianity in any way or form! For Satanism 999, represents The New World Order!
5. Satan's Ministers will not preach against or mock any form of sexual expression that occurs between advocates, through their own free will! For Satanism 999, represents all Sexual Freedom!
6. Satan's Ministers will not preach suicide and death as a solution, unless the circumstances are unbearable and horrifying; then it will be an escape from torturous, degrading, miserable existence! For Satanism 999, represents Life in all its magnificence!

The 4 Crowned Pillars

The Four Crowned Pillars of the Church Of The Antichrist include:

1. Faith
2. Will
3. Work
4. Knowledge

All of these are to be adopted and used with equal respect to the other. Through this combination or formula we shall maintain and spread Our Superior Order of Vampir Satanism 999!

1. In Our Faith is Belief, which is what raises us out of bed each morning or night, with hopes and dreams of fulfillment. If we lose Faith, we lose sight of Our Lesser and Greater Physical and Spiritual Goals and Our Hearts are weakened. We must constantly renew Our Faith, with personal forms of Initiation and Vows of Loyalty, which MUST BE HONORED! Faith is the complement of Will!
2. Our Will is Our Ultimate Strength to Rise Above all blockades and Overcome them and Our Enemies! Through Super-Will The Sorcerer becomes a Great Master and an Organization becomes Invincible! You will all Learn The Power of Conviction! Will is the complement of Work!
3. Our Work is what we Convict Ourselves to every day. We must be steadfast and determined to complete Our Work. When you Work, you must do it with that Conviction and do it as Best as You Can or it will be Worthless and a sign of Weakness. Everything that we do for Our Society, Our People must be

Honored and considered Sacred Work. Work is the complement of Knowledge!

4. Our Knowledge is the Final Crowned Pillar in this Formula of Success. Our Knowledge is built into Our Work and becomes the foundation of all that we Stand For. The Super-Human Children of tomorrow will hold this Knowledge in their Hands as a Great Trophy, a Reward and a Symbol of Humanities Eternal Sacrifice, looking back at Civilizations Devotion to Rising Out of The Primeval Pit of Mortality and Suffering!

Humankind Will Triumph in The End and Humanity will say, We have Won the War against False Religion such as christianity, Suffering such as disease, and Governmental Failures such as Primitive Capitalism! This Knowledge will be a Crystal Key to The Fortress of Humanity and it is All Powerful and as Divine as Ourselves and Our Faith! Knowledge is therefore the complement of Faith!

The Antichrist Soldier's Rules of Conduct

1. Chain of Command
The Antichrist Soldier, recognizes the Chain of Command! Insubordination is a sign of internal weakness and the lack of higher discipline. Your enemies will see your lack of self-control and your disorganization, capitalizing on your pathetic weaknesses. What is a Militia without Order and Control?
2. Engagement of The Enemy
The Antichrist Soldier, will never engage the enemy, unless Ordered by a Superior Officer or in Self-Defense. This means directly and literally, never to inflict bodily harm or to damage any property of the enemy, without Official Authorization! What good will you be as a Soldier, when you're in jail and costing us billions of dollars?
3. Uniform Compliance
The Antichrist Soldier, will comply with the Uniform Codes, while Officially on Duty. What will the enemy think, when you come before them dressed up and looking like a slob, and a lazy maggot? They will mock you, laughing at your inferior qualities and sense of duty, reflected upon your obvious half-hearted insincerity! Are you for real or are you a joke? How serious are you???
4. Satanic Camaraderie
The Antichrist Soldier, accepts the principles of Satan's Divine Vampir Bible, A New Moral-Value System and The Satanic Vampir Creed! These Satanic Morals are designed to preserve Our Unity, help raise and maintain Our Morale, and manifest our Undying Unified Spirit! One is the beginning! What is the key that makes Our Unity Superior, to other organizations???

The Church Of The Antichrist Handbook

Part 1 The Order Of Satan's Vampir Soldiers

Once you join the Church Of The Antichrist you are automatically registered into this Order of Satan's Soldiers with proper rank. One of your jobs is to help recruit new members, though you can apply for Official Recruiter or Circle Master Status which has many benefits. Your other great job is to help defend the Church Of The Antichrist and our Satanic Brothers and Sisters!

This is a solitary order that works together through the leaders of the circles in your areas. This Order is not too religious, though it is mainly for those who wish to support our Church yet have no desire to become deeply involved with aspects of spirituality or Priest/Priesthood. Though, after a long list of members who kept inquiring about a solitary Priest/Priestess Status among the Warrior Class I've decided to allow Priest/Priesthood to flourish in this solitary order. All those who are interested in that Status must apply for it.

Each Official Recruiter becomes the head of their own Circle, a Circle Master, with the rank of an Officer! They can now recruit members into their Circle, which is a smaller branch of The Order of Satan's Soldiers, a Larger Branch of the Church Of The Antichrist. Each new member that you bring into your Circle will be used to value your worth and to elevate your Official Rank! As the Head of a Circle, you get to name your Circle whatever you like, though it must be authorized as your

Official Name. If you apply for Priest/Priestess Status, you will be given the title High Priest or High Priestess, along with your standard military rank. All those that you recruit into your Circle will be given the title Priest or Priestess, along with their rank.

Part 2 The Order
Of
Sacred Sexual Vampir Healers

After joining the Church Of The Antichrist you will have the choice of joining this solitary order or our Elite Order of Satan's Vampir Knights! Your main job in this Order is to find those who are in need of sexual fulfillment and bring them into your Circle of Sexual Worship!

You may apply for head status becoming High Priestess or High Priest of your Circle or you may join a Circle. If you join a Circle you will be given the title Priest/Priestess with your military rank. Those at the head will also be promoted to a status of Officer! The High Priest or High Priestess may use whatever spiritually/mentally emotional or materialistically/physically fulfilling arts that they wish, as long as the tenets of my Satanic Bible are followed. They can teach these methods to the members of their Circle.

Again, as the head of your Circle as Circle Master, you can name it what you will, yet it must be authorized as your Official Name! The Sacredness of this order must be emphasized and not forgotten. You are providing a service to The Satanic People, because Sexuality is more than a desire, it is a NEED that must be fulfilled in order for a Human Being to be healthy. Also, since you are providing such a great service to Humanity, you must be Honored, Respected, and Glorified! Hail The Holy Whores' of Babylon!

Part 3 The Order Of Satan's Vampir Knights

After joining the Church Of The Antichrist you will also have a choice of joining this Order. This is the Elite Order of Satan's Knights of Valor or The Knights of The Temple! This Order is dedicated to defending the Temple itself and protecting, teaching, and spreading the Sacred Principles of my Satanic Bible.

This is an Order of Warrior-Priests and Warrior-Priestesses. We not only train in The Martial Arts, we train in the Religious/Magickal Arts and The Official Arts and Ceremonial Rites of this Temple. Since, this is an Elite order, there is only one High Priest or First Priest and that is myself. Also, all rules must be followed completely or excommunication from the Church Of The Antichrist will ensue or expulsion from this Order! This also, is a very Sacred Order. The members of this Order hold the highest Honor, Respect, and Glory and must be shown such Respect, Honor, and Glory! As for applying for Circle Master Status, you will be given the title Vice-High Priest or Vice-High Priestess! Special rules apply and other initiative rank and titles will be used as well.

Part 4 Circle Master Application Regulations

1. You must serve one year in a Circle, before you can apply for Circle Master Status!
2. You must have at least five members ready to join your Circle or have five join in one month!
3. You must either have Officer Status or be accepted and granted Officer Status!
4. You must have or build your own website promoting the Church Of The Antichrist!
5. If you fail these rules you must wait one year before reapplying for Circle Master Status!

The Definitions
of
A Satanist 999

1. You must support the complete overturning of the judeo-christian moral-value system! This makes you a true adversary of judeo-christianity. The ancient semitic word for adversary or opponent is Satan! Therefore, as a true adversary, you come as a true Satan against them!
2. You must support My New Left-Hand Path Moral-Value System, The Philosophy of 999! This creates balance and stabilization where there is confusion, destabilization, imbalance, and emptiness, filling the void!
3. You must support Satanism 999 as a real Religion and not some pseudo-anti-religion! Satanism must become Satanism 999! As a real religion, you must accept Satan as a real divinity within yourself or creation! Therefore, you must accept the term Satanist 999!
4. You must support the formal organization of Satanism 999, within the Church Of The Antichrist! This is the formal organization of a legitimate Priest and Priestesshood, dedicated to Satanism 999, as an actual dignified religion! This formalization will give Satanism 999 a true and solid foundation to build upon and grow! This excludes other organizations that may work against the goals of the Church Of The Antichrist! Through a solid foundation I swear that Satanism 999 will have a long future ahead and we will be freed from judeo-christian oppression!
5. You must support all Left-Wing concepts and principles set forth by the Church Of The Antichrist! This excludes all right-wing judeo-christian concepts and principles! Many of these Left-Wing principles include, the true natural rights to gay

marriage, gays in the military, prostitution, pandering, drugs, abortion, capital punishment, Etc.!

The Precepts of Salvation

1. Life is always greater than death, unless death is escape and freedom from living hell!
2. Divine Family is always greater than common family and self, unless Divine Family takes away your true freedom!
3. Health is always greater than wealth or money and power, unless wealth secures your Health!
4. Peace is always greater than war, unless war is unavoidable and it is a last resort to securing true freedom and Eternal Peace!
5. Spirit is always greater than law, when law has stolen your true rights and freedom, unless Spirit allows law to exist!
6. Love is always greater than hate, unless hate must rise in war!
7. One Unity is always greater than many, unless One enslaves your true rights!
8. Sexuality is always greater than abstinence, unless abstinence assumes your Sexuality!
9. Discipline is always greater than rebellion, unless rebellion is the true path to Higher Discipline!
10. Purity is always greater than toxins and contamination, unless contamination leads you out of contamination into Eternal Purity!
11. Truth is always greater than lies, unless lies reveal the Truth!
12. Calm is always greater than anger, unless anger brings Ultimate Calm!
13. Idolization and Worship of The Self is always greater than outside deities, unless Idolization of outside deities represent Idolization of The Self!

The Satanic Vampir Creed

1. Beauty
The Satanic Vampir endeavors to remain forever beautiful, yet beauty is always seen through, The Eye of The Beholder! It will be the task of the Vampir to use its power, by creating an alluring aura, which is the beauty of the true Sorcerer. What is within can be seen from without!
Beauty is Youth, Beauty is Power, Beauty is Wisdom, Beauty is Art, Beauty is Soul, Beauty is Lust, Beauty is Triumph, Beauty is Parade, Beauty is Immortality!

2. Anti-Regret
The Satanic Vampir should stand by its own ideals, never to regret its thoughts or actions, but to always face the ax of self-deceit, when sympathy is born! Don't slaughter the lambs and then pity them, out of pseudo-innocence and visual aesthetics.

3. Power
The Satanic Vampir seeks out power for itself and its own or its family, never kneeling to the whims of mortals; the others and will face death, rather than be forced into eternal servitude! If it serves, it serves out of its own desire or necessity. There will always be a master, yet it is better to serve in hell, than to reign in heaven! Choose well your Master or it will choose well you!

4. Lust
The Satanic Vampir must eternally feed, fulfilling its unrelenting sexual lust, draining the souls of mortals! By draining the mortal's power, the Vampir consumes their souls. This turns the mortals into Vampirs during the process. All great Vampir tales are filled with blood feeding, representing a physical desire to sexually embrace the flesh and a deeper sexual desire for the soul, The Life Force!
Therefore, blood is a sacred symbol of sexual existence. Becoming a Satanic Vampir, is not a path to evil, but a path to

immortality. A strong libido represents a great yearning for the sexual life, the sacred and erotic blood of the androgynous sexual soul! This reveals the altruistic and divine nature of Prostitution, Pornography, Polygamy, Promiscuousness, Orgia, Homosexuality, and all other Sacred Sexual Arts!

Part IV Goals

Antichrist Goals

1. **Sexual Promiscuity**
One goal of the Church Of The Antichrist is to replace the Christian family unit, with the sacred polygamous family unit! We frown upon monogamy, because it isolates the partners to each other, cutting off sexual and loving relationships with others. This monogamous greed, denies others of their sexual, loving, and healing pleasures. The future is promiscuousness!
2. **Bisexuality**
Another goal of the Church Of The Antichrist is to raise homosexuality and bisexuality to a mainstream status, delegating the heterosexual world to the shadows and memory! We frown upon heterosexuality, because it perpetuates a homophobic bias and fear. This stigma will persist, until the heterosexual is contained and mentally deported, through the power of swaying social conformity. The future is a bisexual society!
3. **Sexual Healing**
Another goal of the Church Of The Antichrist is to free the bonds of the holy whore, the Sexual/Spiritual Healer! We frown upon Christian societies damning laws and condemning views of morality. We will establish her profession as the second most sacred ascendency. She represents Babylon's glorious treasure and we swear to fill the golden vaults. The future is the end of hypocrisy and the beginning of Babylon's glory!
4. **Local Drug Management**
Another goal of the Church Of The Antichrist is to create and mandate a new system, to determine the status of controlled substances! The hypocrisy of our society ascends to the top of the mountain of glory and descends to our children. They are caught between the tyrannically puritan values of christianity and greedy rich class politicians and military leaders. They will

wage a pointless and staged war on drugs, knowing they cannot defeat themselves. There are no real benefits except maybe to the politician's career. Any economic benefits are an illusion, because job by job, flush by flush, they are draining your money down the government toilets that ironically cost about $5,000!

Doctors can tell you, the most destructive drug of all to the body, is alcohol and one of the least destructive, a simple herb; which is strangely and ironically labeled, controlled! They should be spending your money on better education and devise a mandate for drug testing in order to regulate its use, to its minimum, eliminating and avoiding most legal hassles. If you mandate drug testing at the job level, you create an ultimate incentive not to use. Did you know for thousands of years, the rich have used drugs to pacify their slaves? Their monopolies will be destroyed, through the breaking of our legal chains. The future is solid and acceptable solutions!

5. **The Ascendant State**

Another goal of the Church Of The Antichrist is to establish ascendancy of state law over federal oppression! We can all see it has proven itself to be a machine of absolute self-interest! The future is ascendancy!

6. **Free Energy**

Another goal of the Church Of The Antichrist is to bring the people free energy, crushing the fossil fuel monopoly. The governments of the world have suppressed and controlled the technologies, which will eliminate our forced-dependence on fossil fuels. The future is, Free Energy!

7. **Free Health Care**

Another goal of the Church Of The Antichrist, is to bring the people free health care, destroying the private hospital system and the pseudo-need for insurance! The great irony is, many hospitals are named after christian saints! Plus, millions die, because they cannot afford the drugs they need to survive. The pharmaceutical companies hold the health of the world captive, in their monopolizing grip! Most of these companies are actually owned by greed driven stockholders that could careless about the suffering of others. Here, we are laying the foundation of a truly advanced futuristic society; while they play games in a world of pseudo-luxury, like children at a never-ending party. Though, the party always ends because it is only a temporary luxury. There is nothing wrong with a good party, but we must never forget about the hell that goes on beyond our seemingly invincible paradise. For the poor class, it is always a living hell! So what do the rich do, they make sure there are all kinds of vises to pacify them in their darkest hour. The future is, Free Health Care!

8. **Free Housing**

Another goal of the Church Of The Antichrist, is to bring the people, Free Housing! How can the poverty stricken get ahead when they are forced to spend their simple wages on steep rent, instead of better job skills or professional college education? For most, it is mission impossible! How does one escape the trap of poverty? They must have help from their true Brothers and Sisters. The future is, Free Housing!

9. **Free Roads**

Another goal of the Church Of The Antichrist, is to bring the people, free roads, eliminating the pseudo-need of tolls and automobile insurance!

10. **Free Education**

Another goal of the Church Of The Antichrist, is to bring the people, Free Education! There is no reason why our poverty-stricken children should be forced to work two and three jobs at fast food restaurants, amusement parks, or even join the homosexually biased military, to attain the education which they so dearly deserve, if they truly wish. Is this what capitalist democracy is all about? The education business is an aspiring child's bloody nightmare, unless you're born into the upper class. To make another point, I thought catholicism was here to truly help the people, not drain them of their hard earned wages? So, that is why catholic schools are so expensive; they must be the schools of the rich/ruling class? The future is, Free Education!

11. **Free Food**
Another goal of the Church Of The Antichrist, is to bring the people, Free Food!

12. **Free Music**
Another goal of the Church Of The Antichrist, is to bring the people, Free Music! We believe that music is part of the universal language of the soul. Therefore, it is very useful in helping to heal the soul, or the mental mind! The art of spiritual healing has been with us from the beginning, even though it has been suppressed. This is a very wonderful tool that will aide in the process of Spiritual Healing, even physical healing. The problem is that, music is a business which demands a profit. Most of the spiritually sick are very poor and cannot afford the music which will help them feel better. Our Church will consist of many types of healers and will take on the task of bringing Free Healing Music to those who are sick and cannot afford to buy what they truly need! The future is, Free Music!

13. **Free Clothing**
Another goal of the Church Of The Antichrist, is to bring the people, Free Clothing!

14. **To Secure Our Technological Rights**
Christians are and have banned certain technologies that they feel violates their moral-value or ethical system. These legal bans strip us of our technological rights and oppress us further. They don't recognize our opposing moral-values or our technological rights. It is therefore our goal to fight for, and secure these rights, which will benefit our Great Spiritual Goal of achieving The Providential Existence. We will use every advanced technology in existence, including human cloning,

embryonic cloning, stem cell technology, genetic engineering, nano technology, etc., to raise humanity to this super-human state of immortality!

15. To Secure Our Sexual Rights

Again Christianity has used its moral-value or ethical system to legally ban certain practices that they find violates their system. Once more, christians don't recognize our opposing moral-values or our Sexual Rights and have stripped us of our rights, oppressing us further. It is our goal to fight for, and secure these rights. Some of them include, gay rights, gays serving openly in the military without discrimination from homophobic military leaders or service men/women, gay marriages on the same level and legal standing as heterosexual couples, polygamy, prostitution, pandering, etc.!

Chart Of Organizational Requirements For Advancement

The Essentials

1. The Dream, Idea, Concept, Cause, or Belief
2. The Loyal Supporters
3. The Financial Capital or Equivalent
4. Actual Organizational Development
5. Advanced Technologies

Required Understanding

1. The Supporters must understand that power is the foundational element, to achieve any organizational goals.
2. This power is achieved through economics and politics, via The Political Militia or Political Party.
3. The Supporters must join, donate to, and work for, The Political Militia/Party.
4. The Political Party must be organized like a Militia. You have the Leaders or Officers, the Recruits, Workers, or Soldiers/Supporters.
5. The Officers organize the Party and give out orders and the Soldiers/Supporters carry out the orders and do the work.
6. Many policies must be adopted and complied with to manifest the organization and its goals. So the Supporters must understand that policies are necessary to success.

7. The Supporters must understand absolute dedication to the beliefs and goals is mandatory for success and means dedication to submitting to the work that the Party gives to you to do or complete.

Children Of The Machine

We have entered The Age of High Technology! There is no logical reason why the suffering must go on. Who is suffering? Why are they suffering? The poverty stricken are suffering! They are suffering because of the pseudo-elite rich class of the world!
What is the purpose of the current class society? The purpose of the current class society is to maintain the wealth and luxury of the few, rather than the many or at the expense of the many. Every time you support capitalist/democracy, by voting, joining "The Official Military," etc., you support this economic class system. By supporting that system, you empower the rich class and outcast those that are literally forced into poverty, "The Poor Class or Lower Class!"
Those of the rich class have devised a smoke screen, shield, or magic curtain, to hide the unchanging and growing effects of the poverty they enforce upon the majority of the people of the world. They do this through controlling the media, turning activists into terrorists, using covert operations to subdue opposition to their elite order, etc., and when all else fails, they call upon their rich class war machine, "The Official Military!"
What kind of society allows thousands of its people to be laid off without any compensation, by corporations that have just decided to move to a more economically productive location? No true society!
Then what kind of government allows this to occur? A very uncaring and self-motivated government, a corrupt government! There is no true peoples' government; there is only a rich class government!
The Age of The Machine is upon us. The computer now runs society, rather than man. This is a beautiful concept, because a computer cannot be corrupt, only its program. If the rich class

controls the program, then it will be a corrupt machine, a corrupt god. If those of the poor class control the program, the machine will delete the corruption, eliminating poverty!
We are the Children Of The Machine and the race has already begun. Our children's children will never know poverty or a corrupt class society! Join the valiant fight, against the true evil! The Dawn of The Apocalypse is here! **Children Of The Machine Unite!** (Evil as in the greater wrong and True as in the closest right!)

Religious Organization and Network

As part of our ever expanding and further development of our Religious Organization and Network, we will need to lay the groundwork for parallel institutions to counter our enemies sinister clutches on the people of society.

They have been using religious, olitical/economic, military, medical, psychiatric, psychological, etc., institutions based around religious cores to dominate and oppress everyone with opposing moral-values in this morally/ethically homogenized society that they've created.

Therefore, I am announcing the formation of institutes that will be erected over time to counter every aspect of their oppressive imperialist regime.

We will hereby be organizing The Satanic Religious Association, The Satanic Political/Economic Association, The Satanic Military Association, The Satanic Workers Association, The Satanic Medical Association, and The Satanic Psychiatric/Psychological Association,

The Satanic Artists Association, The Satanic Lawyers Association, Etc.

In these Associations we will gather together many supporters of the beliefs and goals of our Church, uniting them under our banner, working toward the highest social powers and control. We will also be working on the joint development of The International Satanic League, The Satanic Educational Institute, The Satanic World Peace Party, Etc.

If you would like to participate in the development of any of these organizations that are absolutely necessary, then let us know immediately. Nothing will happen over night! Be prepared for a long drawn out campaign to erect our establishments and to draw any power or control for our uniting people.

We are obviously looking for Satanists/Vampirs, Antichristians, Politicians, Economists, Trained Officers/Soldiers, Labor Union Bosses/Workers, Medical Doctors, Psychiatrists/Psychologists, Artists/Musicians, Lawyers, Teachers, Scientists, Technicians, Etc.

Sincerely,
Caesar 999

The New World Economy

Welcome to my Church Of The Antichrist! Since most of you were a child you were spoon fed two very different tastes, one bitter, the other very sweet.

First the bitter, I'm talking about the right-wing moral-value system of judeo-christianity. This system is undoubtedly on the surface, spiritually representative of the good of the whole or interdependence, which isn't exactly bad by itself. Then they overlap that with an independent social-economic system, the sweet to many especially the rich.

We live in a world economic system, not just a country or national economic system. What we do here affects everyone else in the world.

There is a world economic ladder. In order for the rich to be at the top, the poor must remain at the bottom, which is three quarters of the world! This take care of your own philosophy has allowed the rich or ruling class, to prosper. They have used christianity as an aid to subjugate the masses through religious/political intervention.

Therefore, christianity has always been and always will be a weapon used to attain and stabilize power. It has been the ruling class's ace of spades. The moral-value system itself is meaningless to the ruling class. Hypocrisy can be a King's best friend or worst nightmare.

Though it is essential for them to maintain their weapon, in helping the true christians maintain their moral-value system throughout. The goal of The Church Of The Antichrist is to completely overthrow that system, which can't be done without overthrowing those who support and maintain that system!

The first step toward this goal is to understand the greater power of interdependence, which does not mean forgetting our independence.

This only means, we must regard our independence as secondary to the good of the whole in order to accomplish our united goal. Don't think for one moment that this means giving up what you own or the right to owning and running your own business! This simply means, in heart, you know what comes first and you know why! This also means a difference in social/economic policy, but as I said, it doesn't take away, only adding to an imperfect system. This is a start toward a new world economy!

Part V Rituals and Ceremonies

The Holy Initiation: Sacrementum

(This is the sacred initiation oath of Satan's Vampir Knights!)

The purpose of my life is Order and to be forever ordained to this Order I have chosen. I am a living sacrifice, for I have dedicated my life to this Order. Since the Creator has vowed to create this Order and has proven so, and has done so out of His/Her love for me, I to vow to stand by and assist the forever continuance of this Order.

This Order is the Order of Life and Death and I shall be reborn to it. My life is a caldron of eternal existence, hence my death only a bridge that spans the voids of reason. Be it for me, the world given by the God of Self and shall I seek only that what I need to survive. Through these words I declare to protect this world from all those who seek to destroy it and our children. At last, I have seen through the fiery eyes of the Dragon and He/She hath declare me a Soldier of Truth and so I shall lay down my life before the Order of Judgement. I hereby take my seat adjoined, One with this Holy Order. Through this Oath I submit to honor the Blood of my fellow Brothers and Sisters, by the same Blood that flows through my veins, "Blood of My Brothers(Sisters) Blood!" Hail! Hail! Hail!

K.T.

The Oath Of The Satanic Vampir

The Oath Of Lust

(This is the initiation oath of Satan's Vampir Army/Healers)

I swear to honor The Cult Of Blood, until I depart from its domain. I hail the power that gives the cult life. This power is the blood of our flesh, The Life-Force. This life essence has awakened me to the true Master found within myself, whom is Thy Eternal Lord, St. Vlad. So upon my knees I swear allegiance to the divine one, myself, and The Cult Of Blood. I hail you, Lord of The Satanic Vampir!

(This ritual is performed at midnight, The Witching Hour. The Head Priest or Priestess and initiate must be wearing their ceremonial garb. The initiate must be upon his or her knees, with their arms crossed in an Egyptian fashion, making The Sign of The Phoenix! The initiate must complete their oath by leaning forward in an act of faith, reaching toward the Priest/ess to perform The Sacred Kiss upon The Sacred Ring! The Priest/ess then places the necklace of the Serpent upon the neck of the initiate. This necklace bears The Symbol of Baphomet, The Inverted Pentagram. This symbol of death, truly symbolizes eternal rebirth, Eternal Life which the initiate reveals in the light of the new day, wearing the necklace bearing the symbol of true life, The Ankh. The Ankh symbolizes Eternal Resurrection, Eternal Life, Youth, and Beauty! By night the winged serpent Set rests and feeds upon its initiates and by day transforms into The Great Phoenix, flying across the Heavens bringing Renewed Life to all of Creation!)

Part VI Satanic Evolution

The Darkness of Laveyian Illusions

I have created my own New Denomination of Satanism, Vampir Satanism 999! First off, I'm anti-laveyian and I have a big problem with these so-called traditionalists. I just don't buy into that! I consider that, all part of the laveyian attempts to categorize and separate themselves from other denominations of Satanism so that they can try and claim a monopoly on what they are calling the only real Satanism. Most if not all of these other serious organized groups that allowed themselves to be called and accept the term traditionalist, have only sprung up in the past hundred years or so and in my opinion they are clearly ALL contemporary Satanist Organizations!

There is a difference between laveyian Satanism and other denominations of Satanism, but I teach people not to buy into the whole, You're a Devil Worshiper and I'm a Real Satanist Bullshit!

That is the laveyian illusion, cast like a spell to blind you and misdirect you so that they may appease christians who say you worship the devil, you sacrifice unbaptized babies, etc., and more importantly so that they can claim the sole rights to Satanism! If they can mentally establish and convince you that they have the sole rights to Satanism, they can continue to guile their way into the thought and concept of declaring themselves to be the only true Satanists, which ultimately grants them a monopolistic illusion that draws to the cos most of those members seeking to be the quote unquote "Real Satanist!" and of course all the profits with their Official Memberships!

My Beliefs can be considered in the light or I should say the DARKNESS of laveyian illusions, to be more of the Traditional BRAND! It would help you immensely to study my Satanic Vampir Bible, Satanic Vampir Creed, and also my Definitions of A Satanist 999!

Satanic Evolution

First of all, I'd like to remind everyone that the true purpose of this christian SHIT coming in here(Groups, Domains, Etc.) is to undermine our goals and slow our progress through antagonistic distractions. Our purpose in exposing christian motivations is apparent.

Our purpose in exposing these laveyians may not be so apparent to the younger and new follower of a forked Left-Hand Path! We are exposing their path as a Dead End on The Road of Satanic Evolution!

They have no higher goals and therefore have no real intention of ever attempting to actually overturn the judeo-christian moral-value system.

They believe that they are not victims, they are not oppressed, and have no true rights! This is outrageous, self-denying and we won't stand for it!

The New Left-Hand Path has been cleared for the Youth and the New Initiate to walk upon and actually reach a True Set of Goals that we have set up to achieve for the good of the whole Satanic People! As for my saying that laveyians not being Real Satanists, this has been misconstrued and twisted by our pathetic local christian enemy! That is what they do, they twist, confuse, and disseminate false information as part of their infiltration and undermining tactics. This is why we must rid our clubs, groups, domains, etc., of them. It only leads me to believe that the mindless, brainwashed laveyian founders of these clubs, etc., are so trapped in the deceitful mercenary web lavey spun, that they can't think for themselves!

How do christians truly benefit you? The level of seriousness by the so-called Satanists in these clubs is zero. They have no concept of Religious Revolution or True Secular Change! If entertainment and basic socializing are your reasons for being here, then you're hopeless, lost, and worthless to any True Satanic Cause! What I said about laveyians, is that they declare themselves the only Real Satanists, out of natural ego, personal reputation and popularity, and out of a need to create and stabilize a monopoly! What I said was, laveyian Satanism is not even a Real Religion, it is just an Atheistic Philosophy. I never said that they were not Satanists. As for us, we are Real Religious Satanists!

Also, I never said I wasn't a hypocrite, though I have said many times, that I'm far less hypocritical for my beliefs and policies. I even state in my Satanic Bible that we are ALL hypocrites and if you say you're not, then you ARE a lying hypocrite! Does everyone here believe in hearsay or do you realize that most of what I say is calculated and what my enemies say is straight up bold-faced accusations and lies???

THE COS IS DOOMED

What's the matter, have the poor inferior and doomed laveyian Satanists finally realized that anton was truly an insecure narcissist, cheap foolish con-man, a weak punk, and an evolutionary missing link or APE-LIKE BEAST reflecting upon the primitive and inferior philosophy he adopted??? Have you realized that the cos is facing inevitable destruction as its membership has completely ceased to grow??? Have you realized that My Policies and My Church Of The Antichrist is FAR Superior to your own CRAP???

Well, get ready, you and your kind have had almost 40 years to prepare and prove your worth! What have you accomplished??? JACK SHIT! The cos is a big sickening failure in my book! It's time for the Superior anti-laveyian Satanists to rise above the inferior laveyian Satanists! It's time to TURN UP the heat! It's time to let the Cunning Jackal out of the bag! It's time to open the REAL gates of hell! It's time to teach you all what Superior Policies are all about! It's time to teach you a lesson known as a FORCE called the Church Of The Antichrist!

The elite of the cos is nothing more than a fancy title for a bunch of low-life mercenaries, who are doomed to an anti-social undercurrent.

They are just another HERD of moronic atheists clinging to a pseudo-religion because they ARE too afraid to completely separate themselves from it. Even worse, they hypocritically cling to Christian doctrines, such as antinomianism! Hey, barton why don't you beg for some more money to save the black house and fill your pockets some more??? The cos is DOOMED! My curse is a curse of Will and MY WILL be upon you!

COS Antinomian
And
Objectivistic BULLSHIT

I've never said that it's impossible to have a monopoly on a religion. I said that no one or group should have a monopoly on it, because it defies our rights to believe in whatever we believe that particular religion to be. Therefore, we are standing against the bullshit that laveyians tell everyone, which is that they are the only REAL Satanists. They tell everyone that because that is one of their methods to building up and trying to maintain a monopoly on Satanism. Well, it's about time somebody exposed their LIES!

As for representing a true archetype of a Satanist, Satanism didn't become a real concept until christianity turned the Opposing Spirit of Satan into their Devil. Then only through the original Christian archetype the truest form of a Satanist can be determined! lAveyian Satanists are nothing but modern day Atheists, clinging to the heretical christian doctrine of antinomianism.

lAveyian Satanists pride themselves on their separation from the christian model, yet reveal another hypocrisy by clinging to their doctrines for support. A religious movement that is separating itself from christianity completely doesn't take on aspects of their doctrines and even the names of their enemies. This must be yet another publicity tactic! Doctrines like that must die with the church and their moral-value system. Any attempt to keep them alive is just a publicity stunt, to enrage the far right to run around screaming heresy! This is great for business, isn't it? If you truly wanted to defy their moral-laws, then you would keep focusing on their moral-value system in an attempt to ACTUALLY overturn it and not just talk about it!

Then lAveyians mix that doctrine with the philosophy of objectivism.

Now, they run around declaring they defy their moral-laws, yet they don't have to fight against their moral-value system and Actually work to overturn it because they are not victims of christianities oppression, they are not oppressed! This is another example of the blind leading the blind, or the enlightened, blinding their sheep! This is another example of their self-centeredness, since they may see no personal benefits in ACTUALLY fighting to and overturning the judeo-christian moral-value system which truly does oppress billions of people, through civil laws!

COS LIES

Now, we are talking about preaching, and converting, which all comes down to a recruitment policy. Every organization recruits to survive in one form or another and if they say they don't they are either lying to your face, extremely stupid, or both!
The cos declares publicly that they don't recruit! This is an outright LIE! After declaring publicly that they don't recruit, they hypocritically and covertly recruit their followers.
Everything the cos and its members do, that publicly promotes the cos or its philosophy in one form or another, is a method of recruiting! This is not only a GREAT HYPOCRISY, it is a far inferior and shabby method of recruitment!
All organizations that have come to any great level of achievement and expansion have done it through open and public recruitment! How do you think christianity got so powerful and far-reaching? They first, used an open and public recruitment policy! How does the military raise new troops? The military raises new troops through an open and public recruitment policy.
The Church Of The Antichrist has adopted this Superior and far less hypocritical Method of recruitment. Besides, I thought the cos was beyond playing on those ignorant inversions of christianity? Since, the christians try and convert us, we pathetic and half-witted laveyian Satanists have to go against Superior Methods of advancement, because we want quality over quantity. That is the most asinine thing I have ever heard of. The bulk of you laveyians should be ashamed of yourselves for such stupidity. Your leaders know what I'm talking about, since they are the ones perpetuating this fraud. lAveyians and the cos, have no higher goals, which means they are all truly out for themselves. Therefore, it means that the cos

is just an atheist's capitalistic dream business. In order for them to survive and pay their bills, they need quantity. Every jackass knows that quality always rises anyway. So, there is another LIE. The cos is truly after quantity, not quality! If they were truly intelligent, they'd stop selling you this garbage and adopt some real advanced and Superior Principles and Policies. Remember, that you all believe in absolute self-godhood, so why wouldn't they be conning you for every cent you have??? I'll tell you the truth though, they will collapse further and then reorganize and adopt very similar principles and policies as my own, because they are Superior Principles and Policies!

Laveyian Demise

It's about time another club or group owner has gotten up the guts to promote True Satanic Ideals! This is another victory for me, since you are partially conforming with my Superior Policies! Your hypocrisy will undoubtedly shame this Great Satanic Deed if you allow christians and other Satanic enemies to violate this True Satanic Law!
Being the laveyian that you are, I suggest you restudy Pentagonal Revisionism! It is the christian infiltrator that you should be most worried about. My goal is ultimately to bring that to your attention and make you realize their true purpose here, which is to undermine your efforts and slow down your progress.
This is a small victory for Satanism on the grand scale and even if you don't get it, at least the Superiority of Segregation through the deletion of myself will be recognized and eventually spread and practiced, yet practiced in the true light of christian oppression through homogenization!
Christians and other enemies DON'T BELONG in our clubs, groups, domains, etc., which are miniature reflections of OUR world environments or habitats! To allow them access to your habitat just for publicity or entertainment is such a great hypocrisy in itself, especially when you delete those who are even greater and truer representatives of Satanism!
In my opinion laveyians reveal their true colors in this fashion, through showing the world that they are only out to personally capitalize on their satanic adornment or how childish and immature they really are enjoying the entertainment that these fanatical christians bring them without ever setting or seeking to achieve any REAL Satanic Goals!
Laveyianism is a dead and stagnate religion, with no true higher goals! This alone spells out your demise and the rise of Greater,

Truer, or more Realistic Satanism with True Satanic Goals for the whole of future Satanic Society!

COS FREES MANSON AND BIN LADEN

According to the Third-Point of the laveyian/cos's Pentagonal Revisionism, it sees men like Charles Manson and osama bin laden as Scapegoats and they should be given impunity or amnesty and set free! This scapegoating is seen as an extension of the judeo-christian cop out of blaming the devil for everything.
Therefore, men like Manson or bin laden become cast as a villain, a Devil! This reminds us of the laveyian satanic creed of Responsibility to the Responsible! In the case of the wtc and the pentagon, all the actual perpetrators perished with their victims, though the people demand that justice or retribution must be served! It is clear from this perspective that judeo-christian ideals influence the present justice system. Therefore, the Third-Point of laveyian/cos Pentagonal Revisionism stands against secularized religious beliefs, incorporated into law and order and calls for a return to Lex Talionis!
This means the feds., the government, would need a whole lot more evidence to go after bin laden and he would be treated as truly innocent until proven guilty of actually participating in the crime itself. Leave it up to the cos to free bin laden!

Lavey Was An Ape-Like Beast

The cos was founded on asinine and inferior principles, by a lowlife mercenary who was a bigger evangelist than any rightwing fundamentalist! lAvey was an apelike beast walking on all fours to his grave, taking his mercenary and useless cos with him. The time has come for a Truly Evolved Satanic Religion and not some hypocritically inferior philosophy.
If lavey had brain one in his head, he knew that his adopted philosophy was doomed, only thinking about the notoriety and fame that he would attain in his lifetime. That is the philosophy he PREACHED from his pulpit, Self-Godhood and everything and everyone else was unimportant.
Now, lavey did one thing and one thing only, which I respect him for, because he was guided by the Satan of Divine Creation. He spread the word of SATAN to the eyes and ears of thousands, but his adopted philosophy is inferior and flawed! The time has come to burry the inferior and raise up the Superior through the Will of the True Master!
If you want to learn more about the inferior cos and the Superior beliefs of my Church Of The Antichrist, come talk to me. If you want to learn some potent Magickal Arts, come talk to me. If you want to hear bullshit, listen to the cos evangelists/recruiters! We all have evangelists or recruiters, they'll just lie to you and say they don't do that. That is so hypocritical and such an inferior method of recruitment.
All great organizations rise up first out of an Open and Public Recruitment Policy. To learn more about cos lies and bullshit, COME TALK TO ME! Hail the Church Of The Antichrist!

A New Satanic Leader

First of all flame-wars are good! They help to create the atmosphere and mentality needed to raise this much required war into a greater field or advance it to a higher scale externally, mainly socially and politically. This war is centered around our personal freedom, desires, and needs! It will be fought with or without your approval, because it is human/animal nature.
Through the study of our animal nature, we develop a science called, Animal Dominion! This science uncovers the authoritarian nature of the animal kingdom. Basically, this means when applied to humans that no matter what, one group of people, religion, or government will always dominate the other. In knowing this knowledge it is foolish to stand against Authoritarianism!
At this time christians still dominate the earth. What this all means is, it comes down to us and our children or them and their children. We will not be dominated and oppressed by christianity. This isn't about right and wrong, it's about our Will to Power, Our Personal Freedom, Desires, and Needs!
Personally, I feel that I represent the most Realistic and Truest form of Satanism, The Superior Satanism 999!
These are admittedly really pathetic Satanic Clubs/Groups, but they ARE Satanic Clubs/Groups. Christians don't believe in magick, they believe in jesus, unless their hypocrites. Those that still believe in magick, cling to the old belief that it comes from their devil, their archenemy. These christians don't come into our Groups to debate and exchange theories on magick, sorcery, etc. They come in here to preach the dogmatic domination of their one-monotheistic god.
Well, their god doesn't exist to me and authoritarian christians certainly will never remain the dominate force on this planet

while I'm alive and my New Satanic Religion spreads to the True Left-Wing Masses!

Also, MANY OF THE SATANIC MEMBERS/SUPPORTERS ARE INTERESTED IN FIGHTING THEIR CHRISTIAN ENEMIES AND OPPRESSORS. They just need the right leaders, like me to show them the way! We don't need inferior mercenary laveyian scumbags teaching them that it's ok to be oppressed by your christian enemies and not to fight for rights they don't have. We don't need those who are not laveyian, but like-minded enough to preach to them the same disloyal bullshit of total self-aggrandizement. We must build a Higher Satanic Unity, dedicated to the good of the Whole Satanic People, yet also fulfilling the Self. We will do this even if you stand in our way.

Through our Superiority, we will completely demolish all laveyian and like-minded outposts and run their businesses into the ground. You will join us or face your own economic extinction! If you wish to learn the Black Arts on a scale above these children, come and join our Church Of The Antichrist! The Black Arts are 90% Wisdom and 10% research! You don't need any books to learn the Black Arts, only if you enjoy reading and reading about other peoples success!

Laveyian Back Stabbers Part 1

You should check out my web site and read all my posts in all of the Satanic Clubs. Reading our site will give you a better idea of what Vampir Satanism 999 truly is about. I will say that the main differences that I see between the Left and right-hand Paths are very simple. The Left represents very sensible sensuous/carnal religions and beliefs, while the right represents totally nonsensible, nonsensuous, and anti-carnal religions and beliefs.
Look for The Definitions of a Satanist 999, The Satanic Vampir Creed, and especially My Satanic Vampir Bible called, Satan's Divine Vampir Bible, A New Moral-Value System! I will say that my belief system is political, economic, and religious! I feel that without any one of these social areas, we will have an incomplete religion! In my opinion, a true and great religion must encompass every area of interest that affects human civilization and the future of that civilization.
lAveyian Satanism, stands against any future civilization, in a progressively spiritual state. We can be highly carnal and spiritual, don't be fooled by the terminology. They represent what I have called Puritan Individualism, which is absolute self-deification, which represents pure mercenarism. This is the individual completely separated from society, as an individual body. This system corresponds to the current capitalistic system which promotes total independence, which ultimately benefits the rich class at the expense of the poor.
Their atheistic system is not a real religion at all, just a philosophy. They are an anti-religion, because they stand against all forms of organized religion in general and as everyone knows, hypocritically incorporated as a church. This is obviously a business tactic. I could go on and on, because I have a whole list of things to reveal to those who want to find a

better, Superior Left-Hand Path! My system does in no way stand against Self-Deification, but we recognize a Greater Deity of Creation, which we call Satan and it takes on anthropomorphic shape within us all as the Lesser deities of creation, but we are always one. Therefore, we are Satan! Also, this is an Androgynous Deity or Creation, reflecting in our own human nature. Therefore, this is a Bi-Sexual Satan, Deity, Creation, or a Bi-Sexual God/Goddess! My system is not against the Self, it just puts the good of the whole higher than the individual. Therefore, my system incorporates a type of interdependence and has real goals that are realistic, for the future of higher human civilization.

Laveyian Back Stabbers Part 2

All of human civilization has arisen from our fantasy ideals and has been the greatest motivation, beyond self-interests that have pushed us on. Self-interests are fine, but when they become the higher goal of humanity, humanity becomes a cesspool of eternal stagnation and degeneration.

This form of capitalistic society actually breeds or cultivates and maintains a poor class to sustain the rich and middle classes. So, they have devised a system that will force billions to suffer eternally. Is this a sign of higher civilization? Do you want your children and their children's children to live in a form of manipulated and sustained poverty and suffering? The core of my system revolves around My Satanic Bible, which is a new moral-value system, designed to benefit the natural/spiritual birth-rights of all human beings. Some will argue that we have no rights, but I say that is based on the primitive nature of this divine world. In that sense, we have no rights, but we no longer live in that world completely.

The purpose of human society and civilization was to raise us from that jungle, to a higher state of spiritual existence. We just took or were forced down a wrong road, with nonsensical religions like judaism, islam, and especially christianity that stand against our carnal natures and self-fulfillment!

So, you see I'm not against Self-Fulfillment or Self-Interest, just emphasizing it over the good of the whole society and making it the absolute goal of humanity! Through LaVeyian Satanism, everyone will tear each other apart, through greed, ambition, self-importance. These things are to be expected in society and are natural, you can't get rid of them, but if everyone followed that philosophy, society will truly rip itself apart.

One of the points of Superiority that I'd like to stress is that of the Loyalist over the mercenary. A group of mercenaries will destroy themselves, through that greed, ambition, self-importance, etc. While a group of Loyalists dedicated to a cause will fulfill what they set out and are determined to fulfill. A mercenary system is very weak and inferior, while a Loyalist system is strong and Superior. Therefore, a mercenary is symbolic of weakness and inferiority.

Many of those who contemplate this will be filled with fear, just at the thought of the Loyalist and their Loyalist Organization. The mercenary to me is the lowest piece of shit on this earth; which says exactly how I feel about LaVeyian Satanists! If you think about it, you're already stabbed in the back, before you befriend them. If you have any serious questions, I'll try and answer them. Make sure you read over the documents I stated.

Laveyian Losers

To begin with, who the hell gave you the rights to the Satanic Mold??? NO ONE HAS THE RIGHTS ON A SATANIC MONOPOLY!!! So, you can take your first rule and shove it up your asshole! Individuality is a given, but that is Individual Character, NOT total nonconformity. Total Nonconformity is the root of mercenarism and it is a big load of shit and the most inferiorly disgusting philosophy ever contrived.

The purpose of human society is to rise from our primeval state of existence into a higher more spiritually carnal existence. You are a mercenary piece of shit, just like lavey, yet he was inspired more deeply by the Divine Creation, which I call Satan! I know more about laveyian philosophy than you'll ever know, it is you who should read MORE closely. lAvey believed in everything I stand for, except my Constructive Conformity and NEW Satanic Moral-Value System, which is greatly needed for the future of Human and Satanic Civilization! lAveyians have no goals, external deity, and stand against all forms of religion and higher society. You represent the lowest shit to ever crawl on the face of the earth and your philosophy is a degeneration of all Human Civilization into the foulest recesses of stagnation imaginable. This is why you are the ENEMY of Humankind and Satanic Advancement and Evolution!

Lavey talked about avoiding the Evolving Satanist, but SCREW HIM! He had the intellect of a clam! By the way, my personal life has been far more exciting than most of you jackasses can ever possibly dream about! KEEP DREAMING LOSERS!!! That is why the cos is on its KNEES, because all your kind can do is dream and live totally self-centered.

I have proven over and over the Superiority of my policies

and principles. Now, it's just a matter of time before the pathetic alien elite SURRENDERS to the True Satanic Allegiance! Hail Satan! Hail the Church Of The Antichrist!

The False Laveyian Religion

THERE IS NO REAL SATANISTS! The ones who claim to be the real Satanists or the only true Satanists, ARE DEFINITELY NOT REAL OR THE ONLY TRUE SATANISTS! I noticed that it's mainly the laveyian Satanists and those who follow the same basic bullshit philosophy, who spread that nonsense about the true Satanist! Let's GET THIS STRAIGHT PEOPLE! No one person or organization has a monopoly on the rights to Satanism as a Religion!

So, everyone who runs around claiming that this is a true Satanist IS FULL OF SHIT! Also, laveyian Satanism isn't even a real religion, it's a philosophy! The reason I say this is because in order to be a true religion there are certain universal prerequisites that must be rationalized in order to be classified as a religion! 1. Your belief must include one or more external deities, outside the human-self! 2. Your belief must include a spiritual doctrine that will benefit humanity collectively, beyond individualistic needs and desires! 3. Your belief must include a higher or greater goal for humanity as a whole, beyond individualistic goals!

Laveyians are atheists and don't have a true exterior deity! Laveyians are mercenaries and could give a rat's ass about the Satanic People as a whole! Laveyians have only one goal that is their self-goal! So, in my opinion, Laveyians are not actual Satanists in a religious sense or do they follow a true religion. They are philosophical Satanists, who stand by a philosophy that lavey adopted! That philosophy is eclectic of course, combining many aspects of different philosophies, especially objectivism and a new age form of antinomianism. Then lavey renamed it Satanism!

I don't believe in most of the principles of objectivism or antinomianism. I find them to benefit the capitalist and only the individual, when we need to be focused on the good of the whole society and the future of society! So, the truth is, there are no fundamental points to Satanism, no one has the right to claim a monopoly on these so-called rights, fundamentals and to claim they are the only truth! This is the same crap that christianity preaches, but laveyian hypocrites do the same thing. The pathetic cos has for years tried to push these concepts upon everyone until you swallowed them, which gives them the edge. I say no more, I'm ripping up the fake red welcoming carpet they tried so hard to roll out in an attempt to blind you from the truth.

So, whatever you personally believe Satanism to be is your truth and if they want to pretend that they represent and follow a real religion, that's their business. Though in the end, the Superior denomination of Satanism shall rise above all others!

CoS Stacks Idiot Upon Idiot

I guess it's true, the cos is filled with idiots stacked upon idiots! Everyone knows that the cos and its self-centered followers could care less about anyone else's rights, that's why you drown yourselves in the bullshit called objectivism! You believe that no one has any rights and that no one is oppressed!

So, it is quite obvious that the cos has FAILED the Satanic People as a Whole! You have no true intentions or goals of overturning the judeo-christian moral-value system and repealing specific laws in question.

You just don't give a shit and that's why every one of you are FUCKING SHIT and I will make sure the cos is pulverized! You are all mercenary scum! It is my Church Of The Antichrist that TRULY has goals to completely overturn that system and repeal those laws in question, restoring our TRUE RIGHTS! As for whining, I am doing more work to attain these goals, than any other group; especially the idiot-plagued cos which is currently on its KNEES!

You say do something and then say why must I turn it into a cause? What kind of moronic statement is that? The CAUSE is the GREATEST WORK! Meaning while you sit here and allow hypocritical oppressive christians among your ranks and play fucking games of ridicule, we are gathering the TRUE COLLECTIVE needed to build political support to rise and secure what is Rightfully Ours!

It is CLEAR to me and everyone who isn't a moron that you have less of a life than me and it is my intelligence that will crush your foolishness once and for all!

If anyone here would like to help out and JOIN THE CAUSE, let me know! It won't be long before the cos is

dissolved and The Eastern Satanic Alliance will be the Brightest Light in the Night and Early Morning Sky! Through our Collectiveness and Superior Policies, we will restore our true rights! Any other way is truly futile and will exhaust our resources, skills, and Personal/Collective Life Energies! Hail Lvcifero!
Hail the Church Of The Antichrist!

Spiritual Egalitarianism

Egalitarianism is a belief that all people are equal or a belief in social equality. This seems to me, to be more of a Spiritual Belief in the natural/spiritual birth-rights of all human beings. We all deserve the same treatment, respect, social acceptance, and access to the same qualities of life. This stands true, provided that others are not treating us wrongly, disrespecting us, or blocking us through oppression from attaining the same qualities of life. Then we have a right, to disrespect them back, outcast them as they do us, and fight against their oppression, until we achieve the same qualities of life or the same opportunities to accessing those higher qualities.
cHristianity and the rich-class do just that, oppresses us, disrespects us, and takes away our opportunities to gaining access to these better and higher life qualities. Christianity does this through civil laws implemented through their majority and belief in their dogmatic moral-value system. The rich class and the middle class do this through controlling an economic system designed to maintain a majority lower/poor class. They also, do this through poorly thought out retirement plans, like social security and they suppress technology so that we are forced to depend upon the fossil fuel industries; which is a form of enslavement.
Now, I do believe that there are many people that are mentally and physically Superior to others, but this does not mean that they deserve better opportunities or better life qualities, just on that basis alone. I believe that there must be methods or a system that will offer everyone regardless of their personally Superior Abilities, a way to gain access to these Superior Qualities of Life! This means that regardless of how intelligent or how strong you are, meaning if you do brain work or you do physical labor, after 20 years, you both will have

access to the same qualities of life. Anything else, is not only unfair, but is CORRUPT!

Laveyian Satanists, believe in Anti-egalitarianism! They like the current system that gives the intelligent the power to enslave the idiot. They like that type of Power, which is nature's Primeval World. They want society to remain in this primitive stagnate state, instead of rising to a Spiritual Apex, which will also be OUR CARNAL DELIVERANCE!

The current system promotes the lowest and most spiritually and socially backwards type of civilization which humankind has aspired to ascend from into higher realms of existence. This system is the most inferior, retched, lowlife, capitalistically mercenary shit ever invented!

The original form of capitalism was designed to help humankind, not oppress us and our children forever and ever, through Poverty Slavery!

Lavey's Heresy

I'm still waiting for an answer??? They have no answer, because they don't even know why, which means they haven't even got a clue as to the reasoning behind the beliefs they adopted. I think they just adopted them because lavey said this is the way to go.

Let me decipher this. They don't know what the fuck they believe in or its origins and the only reason they think they believe in it is cause they have their heads crammed so far up lavey's ass they've gone blind from believing this circus hustler's tall tales from the dark side! Let me clue in the rest of the laveyian beanie babies, etc. Antinomianism is a catholic/christian heretical doctrine, which means that you believe in faith over moral-law. This is a heresy. I'm telling you that the only reason lavey adopted a christian doctrine, is to make christians scream heresy, thus raising his and the cos's publicity level.

Lavey seems to twist this christian doctrine to his own use, by putting that faith in his self-god and defying christian moral-laws. Then they add the second hypocrisy to this formula of allowing christian moral laws to perpetuate, while they capitalize off their religion.

They do this by pumping Satan up, which attracts rebels and then deflates Satan into a pathetic little atheistic shih tzu(preferably pronounced shitzoo). Anyhow the second part is the bullshit called objectivism, through which they cling to an even bigger hypocrisy and lie.

They believe that they are not victims, nor do they believe that they are oppressed in anyway. This gives them the asinine idea that they don't need to be freed from oppression, they don't need their rights back, they don't need to overturn the judeo-christian moral-value system.

This is the most self-centered, self-denial of the reality that I have ever seen. Through this self-denial of their own oppression, the Ultimate Hypocrisy is born. They are using this objectivist nonsense as an excuse to turn the other cheek! I guess they enjoy cowering in the shadows and breaking christianities oppressive civil laws to fulfill their desires.

If you want to talk about Real Satanists, Real Satanists would FIGHT for their rights as a whole people. All laveyian Satanists, including lavey himself, were and are nothing more than lavey's psychic vampires, with their mercenary capitalistic beliefs. They will feed upon the weak, the poor, the sick. They are the true psychic vampires and they must be extinguished in the flames of Spiritual Progress, working toward our true Carnal Salvation! Laveyian Satanism is just a bump in the road, propelling us farther ahead and closer to our true Satanic Destiny!!!!!

Laveyian Stagnation
And
Christian Oppression

First off what they represent is complete self-godhood, meaning everyone else is shit compared to each one of them as an individual. If any group is a spin off the christian ideals of good versus evil, it's the laveyian group representing that evil. And they play it up for publicity.

That kind of mercenary philosophy, which is closely allied with capitalism in general, has only one way to go, that is no where, no advancement of any kind, no raising of society from its primeval state to a more spiritual plane. If anything, it represents a degeneration of society, back into primitive culture, remaining stagnate eternally, without progress. If men and women have no primeval rights, they shore as hell must have spiritual ones to secure. These laveyians don't believe that we have any rights whatsoever.

All of human civilization and society has arisen from our ideal fantasies, which is basically an attribution to our spiritual nature. It is the spiritual that sets up laws to defend our spiritual rights and secure us from primitive natures harm. Though, we also have certain spiritual rights, which are attributed to the carnal. Nonsensical religions such as christianity, judaism, and islam have denied us many of these carnal desires through setting up laws to enforce their dogma, leading us down a road toward a fanatical and nonsensical spiritual system that denies our human animal natures.

It is the goal of my church to not only raise us to a higher spiritual civilization, but to bring us also to our carnal salvation. Under a laveyian philosophy and christian domination, we would never secure our spiritual rights to our carnal sexual natures and our carnal technological ascension into a great humanly divine nature in this world or universe.

This is the question I have for you. Do you believe in your Higher Spiritual Rights, which of course harms no other Higher Being, unless harmed or injured by those others, and unless you need food to survive, or do you not believe that you have any rights to defend and secure at all?

These laveyians will never defend your spiritual rights, nor help you secure them. These judeo-christians will never return all of your rights to you and will continue to steal more of your rights, disrespecting and oppressing you further. It is my Church Of The Antichrist that boldly and gallantly declares to fight for, defend, and secure your spiritual rights eternally!

Laveyian Lies
And
The CoS Demise

Let's sum up what we know about lavey's bible and the cos. We won't even get into the personal bullshit about lavey's life. I'm sure that you've read all the facts.

1. He only wrote about a quarter of his bible.
2. He hypocritically added christian symbols.
3. lAveyianism is not a real religion, it is only a philosophy.
4. lAveyian philosophy combines antinomianism with objectivism.
5. To adopt a form of a heretical catholic doctrine such as antinomianism, is extremely hypocritical, especially for a belief system that is trying to free itself from christianity in general. Lavey and his publicity stunts, but wait they say they don't recruit? More hypocritical nonsense and bold-faced lies. Everything they do that promotes the cos is a form of recruitment. They stand against all organized religion, yet incorporate themselves and claim to be a real religion. More like a Real Business, than a Religion that serves and helps the people!
6. To adopt objectivism, is to say that you have no rights, are not a victim of christianities oppression, and actually means they don't believe that they are oppressed at all.
7. Since, they don't believe they are oppressed, they have no real goal of actually overturning the judeo-christian moral-value system. If they say they do, it's all talk.
8. If laveyian philosophy prevails, then the judeo-christian moral-value system will never be overturned, and the laws that

take away our true birthrights will always remain intact. This also means that judeo-christianity will always dominate all legislation and of course, The Satanist!

9. If the laveyian philosophy has no real higher goals for the Satanic People as a Whole, then laveyianism is truly a stagnate and dead religion going nowhere. They will always remain a minority in society, under christian authority. This is their alien elite, a group of minority atheists clinging to a mercenary philosophy, like a bunch of rats hiding in the dark corners of the world, biting and tearing each others heads
off to survive! Everyone knows that a group of Loyalists is far more Powerful and Superior to a group of mercenaries.

10. How can a bunch of atheists grouped together for support be considered a real religion? How can they ever believe that they will become a majority group? They don't, thus the alien elite. Therefore, the laveyian philosophy which stands against all organized religion is an Anti-Religion, which is more idealistic than the ideal religions! This is because there will never be a world with a majority of atheists and to seek a world that is such is far more idealistic than christianity!

11. The only true way to overturn the judeo-christian moral-value system is through a Real Religion, which must become the Majority! This is the Birth of a Real Religion, Satanism 999! As I've said before, Satanism must become Satanism 999!

Part VII The Eye of Satan

Satan's Sorcery Volume I
Puppetism and The Eye of Satan

Satanism and Black Magick

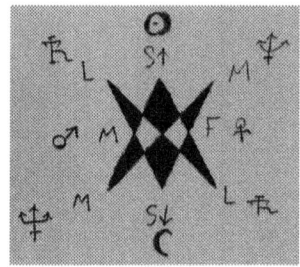

Contents:

Awakening The Beast 666

Satanism

The 3 Doctrines or Paths

Puppetism

The Eye of Satan

Part I The God/Goddess of Self: Revised 2005

The Novice's Handbook of Magick

Awakening The Beast 666

1. In Wicca, Paganism, Druidism, Etc., 5 is the number of man or the human; representing male and female symbolisms. This is symbolic of nature or the human nature. Men and women have 5 fingers on each hand and 5 toes on each foot. We also have a head, two arms, and two legs. If you think about it, it more represents the woman, than the man. ---Many of those groups are feminist based and so it makes sense that 5 more accurately symbolizes the woman. Man's penis gives him a 6th extension as well, to really be technical.

2. In judaism and christianity, 6 is the number of the man-christ, in it's positive form; by three, it is god; or represents god. Christ is a symbol of the perfected man. So positive 6, represents perfection, in a human or male state. Judaism and christianity are patriarchal religions, so you will not find too many, if any at all, representations using women in a state of perfection or godliness or goddess-ness. ---Except for the virgin mary symbolism. For you must remember, these religions lower the woman's social status, to a submissive state, under masculine rule. 6, reversed, represents the man- anti-christ, in it's negative form; by three it represents the judeo-christian devil or Satan. The negative 6, is a symbol of carnal desire and the positive, a symbol of spiritual will, over the carnal desires; according to judaism and christianity. ---This is more accurately understood with judaism and the secret tradition of the kabbalah. Christianity may be using the 7 as the symbol of perfection or the perfected man-christ and by three symbolic of their god.

3. In Satanism, this is bullshit and means nothing and will be sarcastically spat upon, laughed at, and mocked, by the self-believer. ---This is mostly a Laveyian attitude. For each person is their own god or goddess and shall be worshiped, by yourself and whom ever wishes to worship you or follow you. Through all religion, you will find these negative and positive representations, though it is very hard to teach someone a different representation, from the one they've been taught. This is because each person's religion supersedes the other, in their mind, and helps format what they conceive. If someone does not have a religion, they will probably only conceive the representation of the major religions at that time; through whatever they've picked up or learned from them. Judeo-christianity has been superseding young minds for so long it's going to take a hammer, to pound it out! ---Satan's Hammer!!!

4. Vampirism, may be a bit different, but it's also a form of Satanism. This belief system will also, if not yet, will manifest a dual representation, such as the negative and positive formats, just as I teach now. Vampirism, is a further manifestation of the satanic destiny, created by christianities beast. Through their constant condemning and harassing; they've finally provoked, evoked, it into full materialization. They saw their enemy, that did not fully or realistically exist and they forced it to come alive, completely awakening, and now it's going to devour them. For they supplanted the beast in every young mind, watering the seeds of destruction; their self-destruction and raised the rebellion, against christ.

Satanism

Satanism is about belief in yourself and having the freedom to live within your ideal social environment, without interference from an outside power. For example, you may wish to have a capitalistic or socialistic/communistic democracy or nationalistic government, etc.

Satanism is not about believing in the christian devil, even though it is your right to do so and worship. Though of course it is anti-christian based and centered. Satan is a semitic/jewish or hebrew word meaning, Adversary. ---Spirit of The Adversary.

Satanism is the ultimate adversary of judeo-christian religions. For Satanism does not advocate a strict moral code upon its people. This would only be done within your personal circle or family and will never apply to all free Satanists. ---We do not enforce a strict right-wing moral code, yet have a left-wing moral code, which is not forced upon all Satanists. Though we expect our own to support, defend, and teach our left-wing moral code.

Satanism according to my personal beliefs can be separated into two formats. These formats also apply to all people regardless of beliefs. These formats are as such, 1. The Solitary, and 2. The True Group Practitioner. Ordinary wiccan beliefs teach of such a format, yet they don't structure it as I do, with an in depth system and a strong belief attached to it.

Satanism does not have to be too structured for you, meaning it does not have to be too religiously complicated or ritualistic/spiritualistic as many wish their personal form to be. All wicans, witans, witches, wizards are Satanists, according to my beliefs, even though they may claim other wise. Also, all vampires -are witches- which are all Satanists. All or many other anti-christian groups are Satanic in nature and will help to make up The Satanic Alliance.

Satanism- for example if you believe in capitalism- you are The Solitary and you should be free to capitalize off of all those you wish, in any way you wish. This means drugs and prostitution will be legalized, etc. If you believe in a socialistic/communistic society- you are more of a True Group Practitioner and shall you be free to live within your own social structure. My book, Puppetism and The Eye of Satan is set up mainly in a socialistic fashion, though it also represents and supports its capitalistic opposite.

The Solitary Doctrine + No Oath!

1. Believe in yourself or what you want!
2. Love who you want and hate who you wish!
3. Respect those that you will and honor who you choose!
4. Learn what you will and do as you may!
5. Defend yourself or what you believe, and who or what you will!
6. Fantasize or fulfill all your carnal and spiritual desires!
7. Capitalize off who ever you wish!

The Middle Doctrine: 50% Solitary, 50% True Group Practitioner + Oath!

1. Believe in the way of the middle doctrine, and yourself!
2. Fulfill all your reasonable and rational carnal and spiritual desires!
3. Love your true brothers and sisters, and yourself, and do what you will with the rest!
5. Learn of the middle way and be responsible for your own actions!
6. Defend your true brothers and sisters, the middle way, and yourself!
7. Capitalize if you wish or collect your monetary savings!

The True Group Practitioners Doctrine + Oath!

1. Believe in the way of the true group practitioners, and yourself!
2. Fulfill all your reasonable and rational carnal and spiritual desires!
3. Love your true brothers and sisters, and yourself, and know why you hate!
4. Respect your true brothers and sisters, and yourself, and know why you disrespect.
5. Defend your true brothers and sisters, the true practitioners doctrine, and yourself!
6. Learn of the true group practitioners doctrine and learn true responsibility!
7. Do not capitalize off of your true brothers and sisters, and submit all your income, to the group!

Social/Economic Doctrine Status Equivalent Chart

Number: 1 / 2 / 3
Status: S. / M. / T.G.P

T.G.P. Elite: Puppetism + Puppet Power

Puppetism is the belief that all humans will always be subject to a superior master. Every human is struggling to become a higher degree of master, achieving greater freedom from subjection. Those that achieve the greatest states of freedom, will subject many more; these are the grand masters. So shall rise the grand puppet master, whom shall subject all, even the grand masters. The grand puppet master, will be un-subject-able and immortal, un-subject-able to death!

The puppeteer believes that all organizations and institutes exist to subject, the would be puppet. The puppeteer knows that their religion subjects them, while freeing them from another form of subjection; one that they hate!, "The Capitalist Wheel!!!"

Puppetism

I will open your eyes to the light and close them to the dark. What you see is revelation, for you are my witness. Sorcery, subjection, and power; these things are all that exist outside these walls. Here too it creeps in, for I can not lie to you; I am The Master!

All organizations and institutes exist to subject you. There is no escaping subjection, for even the masters' face greater subjection. There is a constant battle between you and your subjectors, for more freedom, the ultimate goal. The more freedom you have, the more you subject others. Every subject is a subjector of someone else. The only wise choice is to choose a worthy master, before an unworthy one chooses you. This unworthy master, will viciously dominate you in a vile manner, as you will be subject, because you have no choice; through your mistakes, weaknesses, and foolishness.

I name this corrupt system, The Capitalist Wheel, which turns forevermore. This system devours its own and turns family and friends against one another. The poor rise up and become rich, subjecting more poor. Then the poor overthrow the rich and subject others with a new system; that maybe better, maybe worse. Though it is known, the worst is yet to come!, then paradise will be achieved. I am just a puppet, yet a better puppeteer. Let the worst come, for paradise is near. Here is my new religion, puppets become puppeteers, subjects become subjectors, slaves become masters, and the dead become alive, shall live, shall rise! Stand on your feet and walk upright. Have faith in yourself as rise together! --- Ascend!

All my teachings come from different perspectives, as they finally arrive here; in an evolved state; a mastered belief system. The road is long and hard. The mind is putty, hardened and pulverized again. Your world is understandable, then confused. You are bathed in paradise and then tortured in hell. You face lies every day and know them as truth. You are manipulated and contoured into a conforming fashion, just by being caught in the system; while everyone else plays at the same game of manipulation. Anyone who says to you, I have never twisted situations to my own advantage, is lying to you; while many lie to themselves. I have said it before and I will say it again, I can not lie to you, my brothers and sisters. I have said, sorcery exists and none can escape it, for all use it; most unknowingly. For I am a sorcerer and so are you. So must you use it to help others. You must use it to work together in achieving your goals. There is one goal that will be accomplished; paradise on earth. No-thing can stand in our way; no-thing can stop us. Believe in yourselves and do what is right to you. Do not condemn others for their beliefs and works; let them be as they are, in their territory, and let us go to our own. Do not let others sexuality burden you, for is it your concern? If your children find themselves outside your beliefs, you must know that they have their own. For you do not control them and what you believe isn't always right for them. Is not part of life about enjoyment and happiness and you're going to take that away from your child, because of what you believe or even what that corrupt high society believes? Your way isn't our way and our way can be, your way. I have come and you can learn.

There is only pain. Let me hold you in my arms and take it away. Your flesh is soft and relieving. My body your vent and vessel, through which you release your torment. Let the negative flow out and the positive in.

Your taste is sweet and fulfilling. Yes, I am a vampire, thriving on your energy. So tell me, what are you, whom thrives on mine? We are all creatures, that live on, through eternal transmission and manipulation of energy. Your tongue is a transmitter, dancing with mine. I love tasting your flesh, it soothes!, it heals!, it rejuvenates! Your hands and fingers are the same, as your touch, is like embracing an angel. You feel like the fresh new born life, which is the same aroma I consume, to live and not be dead! We are immortal beings, that do not age, until the sickness comes. When your blood flows, it takes with it your thoughts and your pains, delivering them throughout your body; like poison from a snake. Then your body, now filled with poison, will die. Though first it shall manifest disease from its weakened state. This disease shall spread, causing other malfunctions, which eventually cause death. Though of course the disease comes from a source, it is able to attach itself on, through, and in your body, because of your weakened state of stability; caused by your weakened mental stability. Your mental instability is caused by your, social atmosphere, your lack of constant understanding, and your undisciplined mind. For everyone is aware of their sickness, just not every moment or you would be crippled by your truth, your constant awareness of your illness. So of course your mind is so willing to forget, in order to move on to another task, escaping boredom; this is your example of your undisciplined mind. For my blood and flesh is one with yours! I will heal you!, I will love you!, I will save you!, The Master!!!

If you desire something and your desire remains unfulfilled, your desire will change, for the time being. For if you can not indulge in one thing, desire, you will indulge in another. Many of these impulse desires brought on by the lack of other desires, will be known as compulsive desires and to the psychiatric world, compulsive disorders. The lack of personal fulfillment will cause a person to enter depression, lose confidence and self-esteem; to be more hateful, more violent, more solitary and individualistic. Every person will react differently, as I've listed a few of the variations and possibilities that do occur. Most of these will be complicated by other physical and mental diseases, such as stress, anxiety, viruses, injuries, etc. We can see the primitive child like and sometimes logical idea of, if I can't have that, well I have this and so to compensate for the absence of the other desire, they over indulge in this one, to compensate for the emptiness, the void like space, in their heart of minds. For their unfulfillments are part of their sickness, their aging, their growing old, their dying, and their endless tears of war. All there is, is pain and suffering; and those that thrive off of your misery. Though they are even blacker and will become dust, black dust in the void. Know me, for I have come, never to leave. You are blessed, with my truth; your teacher, that lives!!!

You do not solve the problem, by writing a new budget or raising or lowering taxes. You do not solve the problem, by passing new laws or throwing more people in jails. This only changes the direction or current of the money, making others richer. You solve the problem by, finding the source of the problem. For at the heart of the problem is the system itself. To solve the problem, you must change the system. To change the system, you must first have control of the system. There are many different kinds of people in the world society and so there must be a diversified world system, that is designed to benefit the many needs and wants of the people of the one world, in which we live! For country and self is and egotistically power based concept, that only divides our one world, making us enemies and creating continuous war. In the past, this was a logical concept, though now we have evolved technologically and the world is too small and too fragile to undergo, greater warfare. Logic now points toward a one world government, acknowledging the needs and want of the majority and not the rich few, who dictate world policies. So it is time, for us to bring up our moralistic/spiritualistic side, to meet with our new logic. Let us bring up the rear, the head has been waiting. This isn't a moralistic fanatic creature, that deals with sexual conduct or petty capitalistic desires; it's a creature of basic good intention, for the whole of humanity. This is a creature that will engulf the other creature, The Capitalistic Wheel. This will take from the very rich, their wealth and from the very poor, their poverty.

The Eye of Satan

Satanism and Black Magick
Volume I

Contents:

Opening Notes

Dedication

Part I The God/Goddess of Self

Part II Satan's Morality

Part III Satan's Power

Part IV The Devout

Part V Evil's Oracle

Opening Notes

I conceived and wrote this book around 1995-1996, when I was about 22 and 23. It is very spiritually oriented and written during the first years when I was still developing my religion/philosophy, and magickal principles. I have rewritten Part I., in 2005, and placed it after the original book. Though I have edited some sections and added some notes. I also added some chapter names. This is a book of magick and philosophy! It is a complement to my bible, written long before it. It is not my first philosophy book, but it is the first concerning Satanism and Magick more directly. I have several more I've already completed before my bible as well, and working on a fourth in the philosophy magick book series that complements my bible. I have many other older books of philosophy and religion I can mention. Starting with my first books and some were written around the same times. The Shadow Garden, The Quest, The Crystal Tower, Heaven On Earth, Unveiling--The Mask of Evil, Satan's Sorcery Volume I -The Eye of Satan- Satanism and Black Magick, Satan's Sorcery Volume II -The Book of Necromancy, Satan's Sorcery Volume III. As I was writing Satan's Sorcery Volume III, I was putting together Satan's Divine Vampir Bible, Satan's Bible, or The Satanic Bible. I also finished the first part of my Vampir Novel, Church Of The Damned, which I had started in the early 90's. These books are for beginners in the world of magick, religion, and anyone who enjoys philosophy and spirituality. I have a few other works that don't really relate to my spiritual or philosophical works, maybe on some level. I have a few song books and a sci-fi novel called Welcome To Zone X.

Dedication

To my fellow Brothers and Sisters,
shall you prosper in the light of Self,
and know that The Dark One is upon you.

Part I The God/Goddess of Self

Chapter 1 The Black Order

This is a statement and stand for those who are interested in Satanic Organization. The concept of Satan has changed many times throughout history. Today our concept is simple, Satan literally means adversary and is the legendary adversary of the judeo-christian religion and god. We are organizing a group of people that hold the same beliefs and goals as our own. Our belief is one that stands against christianity and so we are calling for anti-christians. We do not claim Satan as a god, but if you like, so be it. We are accepting Satan as a national concept to ally us against christian beliefs. We are mainly stating that the christian religion is false and their god does not exist, and that those like ourselves, need to organize. We must bring together our beliefs and create a new social order within our own society. Through this we will not have to convert or conform to a society that expels us and our beliefs.

Man is god and god is Satan. Woman is goddess and goddess is Satan. Satan has a new meaning; no god above. For Satan is the concept of self-alliance. Self-alliance is the new order of man, of woman, of self-god, of self-goddess, of Satan. We are the alliance that accepts Satan as a national concept. This concept is anti-christianized and so we hail the anti-savior. We advocate all sexual freedom and racial harmony. We walk together under one banner; behold, The Eye of Satan; which is the eye of man, of woman, of self-god, self-goddess, and creation.

Since we are anti-christian, we are anti-jewish, anti-moslem, and most other religions. Though we do not believe in their beliefs, we advocate the learning of their religions and authorities. We also advocate the use of many of their teachings, to help our own. The truth is, that everyone needs a concept to bring us together or against. Since we know their truth, being that their god does not exist, we believe in ourselves. They have claimed if you do not follow them you are a follower of Satan and live in sin. We shall use their concept of Satan, which means adversary, to ally us, of course, against christianity. We do not advocate violence and abhor you, you psychotic-devilish Satanists. If you can not believe in yourselves, do end your own lives in despair, leaving others alone. I say to you, place your ego in Satan and erect the lord of darkness.

Chapter 2 The Machine of Satan

Satan is a socialist because he and she does not advocate capitalistic gain against its own people. For when the people are capitalists, they stand against each other for personal gain. If all you care about is personal gain, then you do not care about your people and the goals of your people as a whole. For Satan has and is a goal for his and her people. Satan stands and says, I am the new order, I am the new religion. So out with the old and in with the new. You the people are Satan, for you are the new. Satan is a concept standing against the old. Do not think Satan is a lesser god or according to christianity, a fallen angel, now an evil devil; believe that Satan is your soul-motivation and the concept of supreme unity. Let the name Satan be embedded in your life. Satan just a name, yet a name of ultimate power. For Satan was chosen to become the concept of the anti-christ. Those who stand with me, will drive the winds of beckon. For those who stand against me, you will feel my current sweep you away.

We do believe in using capitalism as a gain against our enemies, the christian alliance. So shall we capitalize off of those who are our enemies.

Satan has become the name given here to creation. For the eye of creation is The Eye of Satan. Satan is both male and female, both positive and negative. Satan is not a divine being above or below. Satan is a divine being found within the soul or heart of men and women; which is the minds of men and women; the consciousness. The soul or consciousness does not truly exist, separate from the body; for mind and body are one. Therefore we are calling or giving name to your-self as a national allying concept, which is Satan. Satan is the name given to self and all creation, though it does not matter if you have a name. The only reason we have chosen Satan is because it represents anti-christian beliefs and we need an allied ego. Though time the alliance will discard this egos symbolic name-head, yet it shall remain the same self alliance. I anticipate the split in the alliance and have only to blame the ego. If you are fighting for power, you have only to lose power and regain your enslavery again. So I say, rise against me children, for you only have to break your backs in labor. For everything has a cycle; and my cycle will end just as quick as yours. To you my followers, let your ego be with Satan and we shall stand together. For Satan is your-self and your-self with Satan is magnified a thousand fold.

Do not fight for leadership, for we are all different gears in the machine of Satan. So each of us will perform a different task. If you let your ego come directly to your-self instead of your ego into the self of Satan as a whole, you will drop a monkey wrench into the intricate mechanics of Satan and cause its ultimate fowl. For example, if two groups dedicated to Satanic Alliance decide to go against each other for the reigns of power, you will divide the ultimate power by placing ego into your-self as one, instead of placing it into self as a whole or the whole unit.

For if you are an arm of Satan, be an arm and be mightier than all others. If you are a leg of Satan, be a leg of Satan and be more supportive than all others. If you are the head of Satan, be smarter than all others. For you are the pride of Satan's Alliance.

So I repeat myself in assurance. For if you are an arm, you are not just an arm, you are the arm of Satan; and shall you be stronger than all others. If you are a leg, you are not just any leg, you are the leg of Satan; and shall you be the greatest support ever. If you are a head, you are not just any head, you are the head of Satan; and shall you be smarter than all that oppose you. For you are the pride of Satan. So shall am arm wield fire, for all shall fear the masked gorilla troops. So shall a leg carry supplies to its arm. So shall the head command the arm, the leg, and the body. For the body connects them all and is counsel to the head.

Chapter 3 A Glimpse At Our Future Economy

    Satan doesn't care what color you are. Satan doesn't care what race you are. Satan doesn't care what sex you are. Satan doesn't care what sex you like. What Satan cares about is your happiness and your satisfaction; christianity takes that away from you. They'll say to you, you have sinned, repent, repent. Then they'll say, go and confess. They'll tell you when you're young, you're gonna go to hell. I told them, I thought this was hell. Together we can fight the social standard of a christian morality. We have the right to have sex anytime and with anybody willing. We must fight the deliberate embedding of the concept of marriage in our minds. We must fight the deliberate embedding of the concept of holy stature or reputation in our minds. For marriage does not really matter, and it does not really matter how many people you have had sex with, as long as your responsibly safe.
    Once people worshiped Satan as a god or goddess and they lived free to their will. Judeo-christianity turned him or her into a devil and the way of evil. I say back, back you christians, do not step on our will. Do not try and control us, we are free and will rise again; in the name of Satan!
If you claim to be a communist and are rich, you are lying, for you truly are a capitalist. They continue to say we are free from capitalism, when they are living in poverty. I say you are still a slave, when you are bound by money. Communism can only exist truly, where there is no money. So will you say, how then will we be motivated? Do not be fooled into believing money is the only way to motivate. Now I will introduce you to my, ten step motivational plan, which will create equality among its order. Each step is a class of honor. The higher your class, the higher your honor and influence or in other words, your power. Each higher class will have greater control and access to budgeted supplies. Your class will continue to graduate as you reach the required level of prerequisites, which is determined by the work you have done and the years you applied yourself to that said work. Once you achieve a proposed class ten status, you become an elder and may retire if you wish at the expense of the alliance. To become an elder is the highest status you can possibly achieve and the most respected and honored title among all systemized classes or the people.
    No one is truly free in any society, for you are all bound by responsibility. So the capitalist believes he and she is free from enslavement, by owning his own land, house, and transportational

vehicles, etc. This creates un-equality and slavery for the poor. For the poor are oppressed by the rich, bound by the money they do not have. For many of the rich acquired their wealth dishonorably. If you are forced into a society, you are a captive of that society. If you are bound by money, you are caught by the limitations it presents you, when you do not have it. For the poor will always be powerless without money in a capitalist society. This means their will always be poor people in a capitalist society. For you can slave or work your whole life and still have nothing, no power, no honor, no respect, nothing in a capitalist society. My communism will create organized and systemized equality and at the end of your work career you will have power, honor, and respect; which equals wealth; which is the complete attainment of dignity.

Chapter 4 One Great Mind

Welcome children, into the light of Satan. Satan is your only friend, for he and she is within you. You are Satan and Satan is you. Satan means adversary, as you are your own adversary. Every one of you makes up another part of Satan. Satan is creation and you are part of creation. So all of you make up Satan together and you make up Satan when you are alone and separate. If you are your own adversary, you will always fight your-self. So on a more grand scale, you will continue to fight your-self. For out there in this world, you will find your enemies. These enemies are the exact opposite of your-self. These people are the ones whom condemn your beliefs. These people are the ones whom condemn Satan and your-self. There is no god above and no devil below. There is no heaven or hell. There is no savior and no soul. There is only your-self, here and now. When you die, you will cease to exist as you know your-self to be. Life and death do not really exist, only in your mind. You are part of creation, so you will always exist. Your mind is where you think and become aware of your consciousness. You could say your consciousness is your soul, but don't forget of your comparison; for it is only a comparison. They say you have an immortal soul and I deny this, yet say you will always exist. For your consciousness is your mind and self is the heart of mind. This is the truth, there is one great consciousness, one great mind, one great self. So when you die, you will find your-self alive, never knowing death. For your consciousness fears unconsciousness out of knowing you will be unaware of your surroundings; hence, unconsciousness. The meaning of life is heightened awareness and in this heightened awareness, we know averagely, we can not be aware outside our-selves and so we have death; a lowered awareness or unawareness. We know sub-consciously that being unaware means you're wide open to attack and are at the mercy of your enemies. So all our fear is, is fear of the dark and what's lurking there in the shadows, waiting to prey on you. Man the hunted, man the prey, man the fearful, man the victim, man the loser, or the lost soul, and the end. The only heaven you will know is the temporary one you create here in this world or I should say, in this life or existence. Go without fear brothers and sisters, for hell is a child's dream; the nightmare of all things unknown. So you will find heaven to be an escape, when we know there is no escape; only to face your fears, face the unknown!

There have been many different beliefs and religions of the past that have had the same concepts and resemblance as the Satanism I am presenting to you in this book. For now it's time to reunite these beliefs and label them all as the Neo-Satanism, the New Satanism. These beliefs have been forced into oblivion by most of the modern monotheistic religions. So like every cause in the beginning seems hopeless and labeled rebellious, whence becomes the underdog of the major social atmosphere and most always an enemy of the existing authority. Satan the underdog will rise from his and her murky bowels and stake a renewed claim in the world of endless war. You can never separate man from his duality and so we find ourselves in an eternal philosophical stalemate. For this is the war between logic and morality, and practicality divides them in a void called no-mans-land. Practicality is where reality sets in and idealism fades, and is replaced by materialism or realism. The reality of Satan is a martial society and the ideal is a pure martial society. The practicality of Satan is that there will never be a pure martial society and never will any society be pure and true to one belief or religion. Therefore the pure partial society will become the dreaded less than pure society that will rebel against itself. So we conceive the almost pure martial society and the true Satanic conformist which will conform to survive, and get ahead like all creatures of nature.

Chapter 5 Evil The Natural Mind

Evil is the natural mind that stalks and captures its prey. Good is the natural mind that sets free the victim, if not devoured when done. So shall the victim value their freedom and the victor, identified as the master of the game or hunt. Outside the social statuses of man is natures wild society. There you will find that very few victims are set free and nature's evil prevails. Though here in mans societies we are not immune to wild society. For it spills over upon us as we are constantly reminded that mans societies are a kingdom within the master kingdom; the wild kingdom. So here too we will find victims, upon victims, upon victims. For man can not escape the wild, as it is in him, in his blood, in his mind, in his being or immortal soul. Man is evil and good. The only good man is the man without victims of his folly. This man would be without food to eat, clothes to wear, friends to love or hate, all possessions, all sight, all sound, all thoughts, and body and mind. For to be all good is not to be man, but pure force; divine force or god. This would be the god of light, though you can not have light without darkness. This would be the goddess of darkness and so we see the duality that can not be separated; and this is the same for man and woman. They say man is created in god's image, not the woman. God being a masculine force, which I am comparing to the good force in which they have interpreted it, is incomplete, as it is only half of it-self. They have egotistically made or called their god a man or male exaltation, though we can perceive the equal forces of man and woman. The goddess being a feminine force, is what they have interpreted as the evil force and what they have dogmatized as the devil or Satan. These two great forces combine into one beautiful god/goddess of self; in which we call creation or Satan, because we are against christianities egotistical philosophy. A god/goddess can not be a god/goddess without the knowledge and wisdom of eternal life and death. For we shall attain this knowledge through our-selves. Eve is our goddess queen and Lilith is her lover, while Adam is their slave.

Part II Satan's Morality

Chapter 1 Drugs, Alcohol, and The Un-American Way

If you want your children off of drugs and alcohol, you must turn them on to sex, safe sex. You must also take away the ability to obtain these substances, meaning you must eliminate the money. The dealers will be pulling the hair out of their heads. We will not be putting people in jail for selling or using drugs or alcohol, meaning we will legalize its usage; though placing a limit on their opportunities for advancement. I have the solution, will you only accept me as your savior. I am an Anti-Savior, because for two thousand years christianity has only caused grief and no true changes have occurred. For there still are the poor and the rich. There is no paradise here, there is only devastation. I have come to raise heaven on earth and rise from hell!

What do I have to do? What can I say to get you to see the truth? This country, the united states of america, was founded on christian ethics and morals. These moral fabrics that hold them together are, marriage, heterosexuality, and abstinence or virginity. This is sexual slavery and not sexual freedom. Everything that breaks these guidelines are considered sins and are Anti-christian. If you believe in prostitution, homosexuality, and sexual promiscuousness, you must understand that you are Anti-christian. They will always condemn you, for their religion will fall to pieces, if they don't. Why should you continue to try and be part of their christian society, when they are condemning you and making you an outcast among them. I tell you the truth, if you are truly Anti-christian, you are Anti-american or Anti-christian government. For they have built the united states of america in the name of the christian god. I call to you fellow Anti-christs to join the alliance of the adversary. For I am the truth, The Satanic Truth. ---They think this is the u.s. of christianity, if america is anything, it will be Satanica!

Chapter 2 Prostitution, and The Legal Drug Solution

Prostitution, one of the oldest businesses in the world. People don't even know why it's illegal. So I tell you again you are bound by a judeo-christian moral. How do they have the right to limit you to what you can do with your own body? First of all, they are the united states government, founded on the christian religion and god. Since christian morals have become the standard, no one looks at it from the other side. They say it down grades or degrades women and makes them undignified. This is only true when applied to christian ethics and morals. For the Satanist rises him or her up in power and dignity. So shall the prostitute be glorified for his or her prosperity and ingenuity. I teach the truth, and what I see is foolishness. For there are true Satanists all around me, still trying to cling to the christian morality, locked down and powerless in christian society. They condemn you for your beliefs and still you run to them, for baptisms, marriages, and funerals. Watch your leaders when they vote; for they are hypocrites too. If you believe in something, do not hide it, go and fight for it. This is your right and no christians or their god can take that away from you. Go and fight for your right to prostitute your-self. For you are free through me, as I am your true religion; I am Satan The Adversary.

By making prostitution illegal, you are violating our rights of religious freedom and our right to capitalize off of our own bodies. First you must declare your reasoning for making prostitution illegal. What you are saying is, you are degrading women morally and respectfully, and you are exploiting women. First of all, who are you to inflict your moral beliefs on a free religious people. Second of all, if you didn't have your beliefs and bias of prostitution, you wouldn't look down on them disrespectfully. Third, men and women have the right to exploit their own bodies. Fourth, you're saying you don't want your children seeing this, because of your beliefs. While our beliefs teach that there is nothing wrong with sex and if you can support yourself through having sex with others, more power to you. Fifth, the more you try to hide something the more they'll want to see and do it. There will always be prostitution, and in the areas where it is outlawed, you'll find more rapists.

We must legalize certain drugs, for there will always be drugs and a market to sell them to. We must impose a control system and limit sales. We must have mandatory tests at work, so that you can ensure those who use drugs, will never go beyond a certain class of job and or pay. For this imposes limitations, walls in their paths to success. This will deter eighty percent of users. For just like drugs there will always be users of those drugs. This will clear out the jails of needless imprisonments.

Chapter 3 Capital Punishment, Homosexuality, And The Pseudo-Xtian

Those that use capital punishment as a determent for murder, etc., must declare, yes we are hypocrites and this is vengeance. So must they televise these executions and send the money back to help balance their federal deficit. This is logical thinking and the opposite of moral thinking. If the moralists have control, they have religious control and are violating my rights of logical religious freedom. There must be a social balance and it should not lean or tilt to one side.

Homosexuality, will forever be condemned by christian religion. For I tell you they have built a wall between you and them. This is a social wall and they plan to build it with stone. I say you must stand and unite now and build our own wall. For they will cut your throats with embargoes and burn you in their christian purity. Through this I say they will compel you to convert through diabolic tactics. For I say the only thing pure about them is their stupidity. So will you see the light and prove your-selves smarter than them. I tear down the curtain of darkness and blind you with the truth. We are fighting a holy war, a war of faith, a war of beliefs, a war of religions, a war of gods, a war of men, and a war of opposing moral-value systems. This is the big picture, the whole enchilada, the truth of it all. They will not stop until you are destroyed, for they are fully committed and devoted! So, shall you comprehend the magnitude of their purpose and understand your own; which is to fight for your own freedom and society! Through this you'll become dignified and be able to walk the streets with your head held high, and no one will shun you or scream out, faggot! For your true religion is Satanism, the ancestral adversary of christianity. Fools will go and allow themselves to be married by these christian priests and call themselves by these faiths, while they spit upon you from behind their coats of armor, their holy robes of delusion. I tell you the truth, if you are gay, lesbian, or bisexual, they will never condone your beliefs and you truly are people of The Self God or Satan. For Satan condones your sexual practices and will never teach against them, like all christian branches do. You can say to me, well my minister doesn't care, but I know then it is an altered form of christianity and is self-dignified, Satanism in disguise. I feel sorry for the homosexual population that hides its true face under the robes of christian delusions. I tell you if you alter it enough, Satan will climb up out of you and be free again. For now is the time for the truth to be revealed. You can only alter a religion so much that it exactly approximates what it originally sought to destroy. For some christian denominations have almost come full swing, why not cast off your silly christian shell and declare, yes, I am a Self-Believer, I am a true Satanist!---Thank you, Anton, for revealing this fact!

Homosexuality breaks through the veils of pseudo christian purity and frees the androgynous nature of man and woman. For the true god is unmasked in the souls of men and women through the freedom of expression; especially sexual expression. This truth is the Satanic truth, in which we call, The God of Self. Self-enlightenment tears down the wall of deception or darkness and allows the light to pierce the soul. For we shall realize that the soul is the endless mind of god. So will you become aware of your-Self and know, you are God. Androgyny will expose the face of Self and free the God within. If you are living in denial, you are living in bondage and are a slave to your own secret fears of being free. For all freedom is attained through sacrifice. What shall you sacrifice for your own freedom? I have shown you the way, will you not break your chains with confidence and self-esteem? For I tell you, ego is the way to freedom, beginning with the self within and slowly climbing out from imprisonment. Though I warn you not to get too far ahead of the Self, or you will lose the Self and your Ego will be left alone to fend for himself to drown in arrogance, which leads to more ignorance; the sign of weakness. I tell you if you are made an outcast, go and form your own society and turn the tables on them, by making them an outcast in your society. For they will suffer as you have suffered.

Chapter 4 Promiscuousness, Monogamy, And The Rise of Bigamy

Promiscuousness and monogamy is what this lecture is about. So like how it is your choice to have a certain sexual preference, it is your choice to be promiscuous or monogamous. Though I believe that marriage is a trap for fools, it is your right to get married, if that truly makes you happy. I also believe that it is your right to announce openly and have a large open wedding, so that others bare witness to your bond. Though I also see this as a lack of faith in your-Self. If you make a private monogamous bond, you should believe in it and stand by it, telling others, no I am taken or married. If you can't do that you should not take any oath. The most pitiful thing about it is, the law giving powers have stepped in taking control. First they made bigamy illegal, because it formats a certain communism and again defies christian stature and morality. It is our right to be bigamous! So it comes down to what I believe is, marriage should be a mutual private bond or oath made between as many partners as you wish. Though if you want a big open shebang go right ahead, even though I see that as a lack of Self-assurance. Also, the law givers that is those in power, have no right in making bigamy illegal. You must remember that you the people put them in power, through your votes. Obviously, now there is a christian majority. Another reason I believe in a form of bigamy is because in a close group, you can care for each other and have much safer sex, because if you care and respect your partners, you will be willing to take tests and only have sex with those in your group or those you have mutually approved. This kind of bigamous group will ask those they like to be tested before entering or joining the family. To join the family would be like marrying into the family, through oath or bond; this is a form of bigamy. So I tell you, follow no law that they've set up in these matters, don't sign any documents, and don't go before any christian priests, to be married. For I say, then you will have joined them and are my enemy, the enemy of Satan. So I say, go and be promiscuous, and have sex with everyone you wish, for the day will come and we will come to power and we will lower the legal age of sexual consent. Then we will be free from christian dogma! Though at this very moment you can be free to many wives and husbands. For if you both agree to a bond and take an oath with your-Selves, you are married or bonded. Then shall you say to others, we are married. I tell you no matter what they say they can't take that away from you. The same is with your name, for remember it is your name and you can do with it what you will, logically.

Chapter 5 Guns, Anarchists, and Holy Wars

The purpose of the gun is a weapon of war. Do you understand the rules of war; there are no rules. First it is used as a tactical advantage to intimidate and deter your enemies. Second, it is your superior weapon of self-defense. Third, it is your alternative form of entertainment. Forth, it is the masterly hunting weapon of choice. For every tool is a weapon and every weapon a tool. This world is wild and no one ever completely safe. So all weapons of defense and offence are at your disposal, as will your will be. Your most powerful weapon is your intellect and experience or in other words your wisdom. If the anarchists had their way completely the world would be seen more in perspective than it is now. For to escape nature is to escape our-selves. This would be the greatest wake up call, to the wild. For if we don't create the perfect sanctuary, we will only be creating a den for beautiful and natural chaos. So must we endeavor to create, a heaven on earth, even though I am in love with chaos in its pure sense. I know that fear is your friend, which at times you must fight and death is your fate, which at times you must defeat. So I tell you, you are immortal, must you only know why you die? If you're filled with faith, you must be filled with life and if you are filled with doubt, you must be filled with death.

So like the sword, shall the gun perish as the new replaces the old. For greater knowledge, greater magick always prevails. Though I say there will be a lost kingdom that revises the sword and so the gun, laser, and sonic wand will be forever etched into history. I say man will always play, but when he plays too much his enemy will be working and working to defeat him. So shall your enemies hit you in your sleep. I say to you, go and be educated and trained for war. All your training is preparing for war, no matter what you're told. Everything you do for profit is everything you do to get over, over your enemies. For the rich overpower the poor and the poor overpower themselves. This is the grand truth! This is my truth! I tell this to you, every day you are fighting and every day you are winning over others, yet still losing to many more. If you truly love your own people, you would not capitalize off of them. For I say, go capitalize off of your enemies. Your enemies are all those who will not join us and our religious war. Yes we are fighting a holy war and people will die as men and women divide, to take up sides. So you say, how can you be fighting a holy war? Holy is a word that brings forth the union of people to be pure and true to their own belief. So shall we be impenetrable and impeccable. Our war like all others is religious, for what you believe is your religion.

Chapter 6 The Road

    The day was cool and windy. A storm was brewing. All the towns people were in a state of uneasiness, and the animals were disturbed. Then around midday a call was yelled out from the watch tower. "Behold Satan has come and his army is greater than the stars in the heavens." All the people started shouting and screaming, many cries were heard. For now they know that death is upon them. Then another yell came from the watch tower. "Behold it is Leviathan and his army is greater than the drops in the sea." So the people cried out even more, pulling the hair from their heads and tearing their clothes, for now they know that doom is upon them.

    Then some people stood by each other and said, let us go out to Satan and tell him we swear allegiance to him and maybe we will be spared. Then another group of people stood by each other and said, no, let us go out to Leviathan and tell him we swear allegiance to him and then maybe he will spare us.

    The arguing grew until neighbor went against neighbor and house against house. All the people began to fight and wage war in the streets, that were plagued to death and doom. Stones flew through the air and swords clashed and fires raged. Children were trampled by horses and women raped in the alleys. Terror was all that reigned in this ruin of a town.

    So now some rode off to meet the two armies and I went to meet Satan. I looked back and seen the smoke of chaos and plunder rising. We approached them slowly as terror creeped up our spines. They all sat upon horses and they stretched back as far as the eye could see. For they are the road of victory.

    What creatures are these I thought as we approached. We got down off our horses so that we could express our lowliness and shame. Then, it was then that I seen their faces, what horror has come upon us? They were beasts of death with gorilla faces or masks and they screamed out gorilla sounds and mutterings or chants. Then it was he the leader who was riding in front whom then made himself appear to us. He sat upon an armored horse and wore a crown of horns, about two feet long, that rose upward from its silver base that was aligned with magnificent gems. So he raised his sword and said kneel with the voice of power. Then miraculously the entire column of soldiers fell from their horses and laid prostrate to him. I say it was then that my legs could no longer hold up my body and my fear laid me on the ground, along with my other companions. They began to make gorilla sounds again and started to grab at us, and touched us and none of us could speak no more. So it was then I noticed the road, the great road that led from the ends of the earth toward the town. I looked again and there was gold bricks piled around me and half the road was already laid out and I looked toward the town and seen the dirt road go beyond it forever. He then spoke while he pointed and said, start here and here and here, then he began to laugh insanely and so his soldiers joined him. I looked again and saw workers working all along the road laying bricks and then I saw they were not really bricks, they were skulls cemented side by side and laid atop bones. Then I realized that this is the eternal road of death and so must there be an eternal road of doom, and they are one. So we are all plagued with and shall slave and die along, the road of progress.

    So believe my children, believe in your-selves. For eternal peace does not exist, only in your mind, in your believing mind. For there is your true paradise with beautiful music and colorful lights. Here in this material world you'll only know a temporary state of peace, for everything is always in motion and can never stand still nor remain the same. For we are at endless war with ourselves. No one can say, if you believe it will be, but only if you all believe. This is irrational, for everyone is different and no one person or belief is the same or ever will be the same. So, I tell you the truth, we have been forsaken by our own indifference and bigotry. For we are deemed and doomed hypocrites, as we keep trying to escape nature, only in annihilation and maybe not even then. The anarchists natural truth kill or be killed, take what you need or want or it will be taken from you, destroy all of your enemies or they will rise against you! The communistic dream of a one world nation with no or a pure/sacred class system is the most beautiful concept ever imagined. For this can only be achieved through annihilation of all your enemies. I say this nation will last a long, long time and a state of paradise will be achieved. Then will come nature to rise us against each other and prove its dominance over humanity.

Chapter 7 Class Submergence, The New Society,
And
The Ego Vampire

There will be those that say society can not exist without a class status, like I said, anything is possible- for a time. This is the key for everything- time the endless theory of evolution. I say to you, children of earth, welcome to your own experiment; nature is counting on you. Go and succeed through your-Self. Rise from dust, set them on end and make your power known to the world. For your life is only meaningful to your-Self and what you work for now will be honored tomorrow in the land yet to be born. For your name will make it-Self known through your chosen sacrifice.

To rise above you must come from below and below you are your ancestors. To achieve this you must be fully educated and by this you sacrifice your play, your desires. Everything you do and say emanates spiritual power and it will grow into something potent and complete. I say go and forge the sword of power and raise it to victory in the name of The Fiery Truth. I baptize you in The Fire of Satan; The God of Self.

I despise you, with every waking thought. My whole life has been affected, by your carelessness. You should have prepared for me, the riches of kings, and succession to the crown on the throne of glory. This is what I come for and nothing less will I accept. There is no selfishness or greediness in the eye of nature. For all there is, is man pillaging to survive in a world that was here millions of years before him and will still be, millions of years from now. Do not believe that modern man is modern man, because we are still infants to the cosmos and our knowledge yet to be born. What we know is still minute compared to what's really out there. The truth is we'll never know everything and always pretend we do. So don't let your leaders tell you, this is the right thing to do and this is the wrong thing to do. Let your judgement decide whether to allow such things to be outlawed or just limited. I tell you the truth, man is going to form two distinct groups with many sub-groups. Then from these fashions will strive to push back and or overcome the other. This will cause the ultimate colonization of space. For colony will try to escape colony and religion from counter religion. War will escalate and resources will be the link and key to control. Space will provide these new habitats and become the source of resources.

For you will all envy me, sought after what you were not willing to sacrifice for and you will despise me for what I do, brings you to ruin because you have adapted to it and conformed your-Self to that society. This is like someone that hates a society and the government, then they turn around because of your intelligence and start a profitable business. Then comes along someone willing to put in the time and energy to fight for what they believe in and it's the same thing you believe in, but now it jeopardizes your business and way of life. So I create a double negative in your book, because you were not willing to stand up for your rights and face the supreme authority. Since I made the sacrifice and chose to fight for the underdog instead of just conforming to the authority and or religious authority, I become a greater outcast and so your double standards help fuel the fires of opposition. Through your crooked two faced beliefs you sharpen the double edged sword. Then when everything seems lost for you, I know it won't be long before you join me and conform to the new society. For the farther you push me outside of your social walls, the greater you fortify me within my own new social walls. This is because if you are accepted by one, you will be unaccepted by another and vice versa. So as one takes acceptance away from me another will be giving it to me as an equal balance. The more you take from me, the more will be given and the more you give, the more will be taken. So my power will grow as you take from me and I will rise up and unleash my sorcery upon you. For you will know my power even in death. Hence forth, The Satanic Conformist, will be born again just as was before, in times of old. You can not stand up for just any cause and expect this sort of domino effect. There must be a superior cause and it must be the exact opposite of what your fighting. For balance is the eternal key, so I await you as you step forward up onto the scales of harmony. For if you are positive, your enemy is negative and if you are negative, your enemy is positive. If your enemy is the same as you, you will be dividing your power and facing a lost cause as you find enemies surrounding you instead of in front of you, hence, the front of war. So shall you understand, The Satanic Alliance, with its combined beliefs named after what they truly and almost exactly stand for. Since Satan is their greatest adversary and since all these different beliefs are associated with Satan, why not call it Satan? We are not saying that Satan is a God or Devil, we are using this name as an identification to recognize our own, and they already have identified us with Satan.

The ego vampire, is one that constantly puts you down, degrades, makes fun of you, and disrespects you. Most of these leeches and con-artists prey on the already insecure and those that lack confidence in themselves. They constantly put you down, boosting their ego up, while getting a high. They will probably keep using you through your naivete until you have nothing of value left, then they will move on to their next victim. ---- Thank you, again, Anton!

These ego maniacs are addicts of their own ego and so will endlessly manipulate their victims for the high and material spoils. They are plagued with their own false pride and so deep within most are more insecure than others. Since they fear their own insecurity, they will continue to put their victims down to increase their ever depleting ego. So will they be faced with greater and greater challenges to keep their false pride from collapsing; hense revealing their inner truth or hidden truth. The ego masters will be able to put down hundreds of people at the same time, through the media and other mass outlets.

This insecurity will only be a disguise to many ego vampires that are far advanced and unique from the majority. For they understand the ego and may never show signs of insecurity and then suddenly and purposely reveal them at the right time so when their victim begins to stand up for them-self, these signs come out slowly and changes the victors whole persona, while confusing the victim. I will say there are many types of vampires and many are naive of them-selves. This is part of the magick or science, the psychology of the individual and so will begin a philosophical vampire hunt. All vampires are sorcerers and most do fall towards the more fiendish stereotypes.

The truth is that your enemies won't always be your enemies and at times will be your friends more than your friends. So will you help your enemies, when the time of fate twists into a new reality and destiny has a hand at oddity and humor. For the truth is only to good to be true as your enemies are not your enemies, yet only your other half come against you and you against your-Self. So through the magick and majesty of life we so terribly equate and captivate in and as time, shall learn our Self-worth. What I say is this, none shall survive without the book of logic and none will believe this without the book or moral. If you cut off the hand that feeds you, will you not starve? If you gouge out the eyes that guide you, will you not become lost? If you are found guilty of a crime, will you not be condemned? So I say if you do not use your rationality and be logical, you will starve, become lost, and die. What you must not forget is your own vampirizing ego, that puts others down out of spite, arrogance, etc., which leads to ignorance. Though in fact, these things do not lead to ignorance, they come from ignorance. So shall you learn of the two great truths, which are ultimately the opposite ends of one great truth; the moral and logical, super-being; The Super-Self. So in this book we shall call The Super-Self, Satan, which is The God/Goddess of Self, and is both male and female at once. This Super-Self is you and you are it. Everyone of us make up this being together as we do alone and so does everything in the cosmos, the seemingly formless space and the ever changing matter that inhabits it. What you are thinking is, why Satan? I say, why not? Do you feel jealous and egotistical? Do you think of fire and hell? Do you think of evil and darkness? Do you think of cruelty and death? Do you really care? Do you think of ice and bitter coldness? Do you feel afraid? So tell me, what is better, to live in slavery or to die free? The truth is neither, because the moralist would die a martyr and the logician would first await a time of chance where he or she could escape and then otherwise live and die a slave. So I tell you, this is still not the truth, for this is only two people. What if it was a whole people or nation? If you valued your people and nation, the majority would quickly turn to logic and forget your morals for the time. So what do you get for your intelligence, you get mocked and called a hypocrite by your own moralistic people with a death wish of genocidal proportion. ---This is a perfect example of mythological hebrew history.

Chapter 8 Racism, Illegal Immigrants, Communalism

Racism, the tribal instinct. In the beginning every tribe was distinctive of their race. Every race was allied with it-Self and all others were their enemies. Food has never been plentiful at all times and water limited and natural shelter rare. When your tribe came to a new place in search of these things, they naturally claimed the territory and so should they defend it and your families. What became apparent was the fact that if you want to survive and flourish you must be able to dominate and maintain control. Through this your families would take president over all others, meaning your family comes first. This is the roots of all racisms and bigotries. Through out the years the tribes spread apart to form even newer races. So we end up with intermingled races that have learned to live together as one tribe or people. Many tribes or races have managed to remain mostly isolated in and to their own people. These same people have also managed to remain intact as a dominating force or nation. These people would be the witnesses of their own fabrics being torn from their nations by these other peoples and religions. To them the enemy is the invading religions, races that slowly intermingle and pick apart their purity and ancestral ways. These people would be and will be seeing the end of their civilization. So will they fight for what is being lost or stolen from them. Hate and war is their only choice, to save the remnants of them-Selves. Their people will long for the old ways and so will they try to relight the torch of spirit and blow the horn of triumph as a call to those that can see what they see. They will say that racism is ignorant and I say only when there is no cause left. Racism is logical when there is a purpose, such as alliance. Though you must remember the law of limitations, this will ultimately limit you. For the more you are, the greater you are. So I don't stand for or against any particular race, though I do stand against a particular religion, which does ultimately limit my cause and abilities. This will only make my goals more fulfilling, and so it will you, the racist.

When you're dead, you're dead, that's it, it's all over. For when you lose, the game is over, for you. There is no second chance as you know your-Self to be. So go and win, using the greatest strategy. Don't put down your defenses, don't submit your walls of fortification. For when you are surrounded by enemies you must keep vigil and keep watch. So when they cross your borders in haste, they are by passing your toll and are committing an act of war against you, by breaking your social laws of stature. These people must be detained and punished; captured and executed. For when they sneak past you, it is so that they can get over on you, even as they do sneak past you they are in a sense, pulling the wool over your eyes. So execution is their punishment, my solution to illegal immigrants. For I will not stand for them, taking the food from my children's mouths. These people are technically the enemy and should be treated as such. Now, I will also teach you of the enemy within. For in a capitalist society, they are all trying to get over on you and that is why our festering external walls are breached, because our internal walls are demolished by our internal conflict and so shall we slowly destroy ourselves. I also have the solution, to creating the most stable and fortified internal foundation, which will erect the highest external walls of power, ever seen. The solution is to eliminate capitalism internally. Through this we shall achieve a Satanically empowered new communistic society. --- Legal Immigration should not be so complicated and execution of illegal immigrants is just a way to scare them and shows my anger at the time I first wrote this book. I don't really think that would be good because I know now they are only trying to escape the poverty brought upon them by their own rich class. Also, the rich wanted them here to do the shit work and keep wages down. The rich politicians only began to publically take notice and pretend as if they want to stop illegal immigration after too many hard working tax payer voters complained about them and not being able to get work themselves, and the fact of concern over how easily guerrilla warriors or what they call terrorists can slip into the country, etc.

 What you want is satisfaction. What you want is fulfillment. What you want is cooperation. What you want is defined control. What you want is corporate power. What you want is absolute agreement. What you want is total access. What you want is complete liberation.

 So you'll say, how can I be heard? Who will recognize me? Do you acknowledge me? I want to sell drugs. I want to prostitute. I want to gamble. I want to be free. There must be a place, where I can rape. There must be a place, where I can kill. There must be a place, where I can spin my web. Who will till the fields? Who will slaughter the lambs? Who will pick up a gun? Who will join Satan?

 Even though I do not believe in capitalism, I know the capitalist must be fully freed, before you can fight for another cause. Once the capitalist is completely freed, then you can slowly due away with it through systematic elimination. Everything must go through steps or phases of advancement and can not change immediately without suffering the repercussions, like a fish out of water. These systematic eliminations or changes must occur from within an organized body, that exchanges money for rank and privileges. This exchange will take place over many years and will eventually be forced to engage in capitalistic and terrorist warfare, which will lead to computer warfare, internally and externally. For there will be two wars at once, and if one or the other wins internally or externally, the other will lose. The internal war will be fought between computers. For they will fight inside silicon chips through electrical impulses, along pc boards. The external war will be fought in this world between man and their computers. The computers will control androidal soldiers and mobile weapon platforms. Also cybernetically engineered and genetically engineered soldiers will be sent on special missions. So this ends my vision.

    If your family neglects you, if your family mistreats you, if your family makes fun of you and laughs at you, if your family lies and steals from you, if your family screams and hurts you, you don't have a family; for you are living in a brood of vipers. These vipers are pirates and vampires feeding upon themselves. They shall bleed themselves and drain you. These people are not brothers, these people are not allied and shall fall at the hands of the strong; those that are unified and one. This is what we are trying to create, the perfect alliance; supported by the triangle of magnifico; dignity, respect, and honor. These three things are held together by the glue of foundation; which is limitless responsibility for your-Self and to others; The Great Self or Whole-Self; The Great Family Alliance. The final apparatus to this formula of success is your ability to withstand and endure the hardships of life. For your endurance will strengthen your mind and body. If you strengthen the mind you will become smarter. If you strengthen the body you will have more control.

Chapter 9 Social Nobility

The social standard or more honorably stated, the social nobility. There is the high, low, and in-between though each of these classes has classes within them. People tend to hold others down or put others down by disrespecting them or in a sense dishonoring them. When people feel disrespected or dishonored, it affects their Self-esteem and Self-confidence. The child's entire life can be effected by the lack of Self-esteem and Self-confidence; due to disrespect and dishonor. For these things destroy a persons dignity and Self-worth. The dignity a person holds, is gained as they come into their own or into their Self, through Self-esteem and Self-confidence. People must respect others as themselves, though I teach that you must use your own judgement when concerning the enemy or outsiders. I teach that in our brotherhood/sisterhood, our alliance, we must always respect and honor our own, our fellow brothers and sisters.

If one seeks dignity, one must be Self-respecting. If one seeks respect, one must be honorable. If one seeks honor, one will find responsibility.

What would I be made of, if I let my brain go to waste? After all, in a hundred years we'll all be dead and no one will care. Though still we are humans and we must take pride in ourselves and our work. For that will be your mark, your signature; that which you leave behind. Then if you were great, they will hail you and never forget you. The only hero is the one you create within your-Self. Then it will climb out and others will see and you will fame. Glory be to you of great spirit; great motivation, and great dignity. So shall you master your-Self and be an integral part of our new society. This will be your integrity and standing, upon a freshly laid foundation.

Chapter 10 Fulfillment

Why should anyone of us not have all our desires fulfilled? Tell me, why should anyone of us not make all our fantasies come to life? Why should anyone of us suffer from un-fulfillment? What stands in our way? What is keeping us from our dreams and passions? Who is blocking us from our goals? I will tell you who, for it is they, whom stand against you and your beliefs. Everyone of you can have what you reasonably desire. No one should be in pain because of their desires. This only leads to repressed feelings of compulsion and anger, that will feed the boiler of hate with envious fire. Come and listen to the voice of reason. You must have compassion for your brother and sister, so that they can have compassion for you. Together we can share in a commitment, so that we understand each others desires and help each other fulfill them. We do not ridicule our brothers and sisters for their desires, for we are not children like those whom we've known. These mockers will become outcasts of our society and so they shall learn from you and me. If you learn my law, it will be yours, to teach. If you understand my words, they will be yours, to preach. If you say my name, I will be yours, to seek. They say you are bound by your desires and I say you are more a slave if you are not freed to them. For I am the Phoenix rising again, in youth to rebuild and fulfill.

Chapter 11 Outcasts, Moral Liberation,
And
Holy Prostitutes

One of the purposes of the alliance is to deal with the individuals' desires, your sexual desires. We put away the games for a more mature or advanced system of courtship. The human mating process is lacking organization and completeness. No one speaks of mating as a true art and needed fulfillment for the human expression. Here we speak of mating as a sexual release and not for the act of copulation, to conceive. Most people follow some sort of integral guide lines in their elimination process. These are reinforced by religious up bringing, according to moral conduct. First we'll get past the average norm that was past on by our elders. ---Christian. These include, the young don't date the old and vice versa, the wise don't date the fools and vice versa, the rich don't date the poor and vice versa, the white don't date the black and vice versa or the educated don't date the uneducated, the christians don't date non-christians and vice versa or don't have sex at all for that matter, until marriage, the male doesn't date the male, the female doesn't date the female, the monogamous don't date the promiscuous, etc. All of these force fed subconscious no-no's have been broken by people for some logical reason what so ever the cause be it pleasure, money, power, rebellion, mystery, or simply your beliefs, etc. So, what happens to these people that become outcasts of this socially sexual society? What happens to those who are rejected and mocked by christian society? What happens to the old, the ugly, the fools, the poor, the black, the white, the non-christians, the promiscuous, the gay, etc.? Are they whisked away from the land of oz into some distant reality, where they must suffer alone? No, their still here suffering because that society made them outcasts among them. So they suffer here in this society and not alone, though they are alone sexually. These forgotten people will be filled with hate without their sexual needs fulfilled, to release their sexual repression. For they are repressed and so depressed, hence, oppressed by the society that expels them into a stagnant pool of unwanted-ness, because of some form of childish bigotry and moral constipation, rather a moral liberation. For this alliance is about your moral liberation, from these hypocritical religious fanatics. Here your moral liberation becomes a logical liberation and a step towards sexual freedom within your own social society. Here we do not condemn the old, for what is old? Here we do not condemn the ugly, for what is ugly? Here we do not condemn the fools, for what is foolish? Here we do not condemn the poor, for what is poor? Here we do not condemn the non-christian, for what is non-christian? Here we do not condemn the black or white, for what is race? Here we dont condemn the promiscuous, for what is promiscuousness? Here we do not condemn the gay, for what is gay?

The word whore is etymologically a lover. ---A lover of many. Something positive! Christianity has twisted it into some one who engages in sex for money or some one that is very promiscuous. They see this as something negative and teach that it is something negative. They turned it from a beautiful concept that sparkles with ancient spiritual purity into a modern degraded, dirty, filthy, diseased creature that lusts after every penis and never washed the semen from her vaginal and anal regions. They see her as a roaming phantom sucking men's erections dry like a sinister vampire forever in heat and in need of man's body or vice versa. The word Slut has also beed twisted from its original unwashed, untidy, careless woman to the corresponding religious terminology as some one unclean and promiscuous. ---This takes us back to times of demonic possession and even witch burnings! The fact is, that the business of prostitution has always been cursed because of the spread of disease due to the lack of medical knowledge. So along with prostitution, many people are condemned for their beliefs and actions as they try to raise themselves from absolute destitute, poverty, because it sucks and they are outcasts in poverty. So they can not win, either way they are spat upon and mocked, being held down as the inferior by these psychological mind fuckers. Prostitutes and others like these people should be praised for their ingenuity, spirit, and will to be free, by not buying into this christian purist fanatical bullshit, as it is a mental programming. Yes, it is all programming, from the first second you're conceived, until the last moment you live. This is how you learn and it is, mind control! So if you are a Satanist, remember next time you use the word whore or slut, you are only hurting yourself and limiting your own power. I condemn, yes Satanists can condemn too, I condemn all those who use these words as derogatory comments or statements that lower and disrespect our own and help limit our grand alliance.

Chapter 12 Monetary Charms, Feminine Power, And True Equality

I've said before that motivation is power and the main power or motivation in this society is money. Money is a charm, a permanent material charm, which is a talisman. This talisman gets stronger through your accumulation or more money, and becomes weaker through your expenses. We can all thank Caesar and the roman senate for mastering this talismanic art. This art is based around capitalism, which ultimately divides the people into economic and social classes, that degrade each other through monetary power. These classes are what we would call the rich and the poor. There is no real middle class, only a state of general improvement, that satisfies the ego with a little more than what you had before. Mediocrity is a joke of the highest insult, though should we be grateful and accept our inferiority? For the rich are still richer and you're still poor. If you give the dog a bone he will be happy and nullified to the reality of his master. Tell me, is it a boy and his dog as loyal friends or a master and his dog as loyal enemies or subjects? ---Slaves, which makes them enemies! When he realizes the truth, he will eat his master and will be freed. For slavery still exists when the poor exist. In a corrupt capitalist society every one is out for themselves, creating disloyalty, dishonor, disrespect, which equals corruption. Though it is your right to capitalize in this society, if you capitalize off your own people you are helping to create the poor and corrupting your own people as a corrupter. This means you are truly against each other and have no true alliance. To create a true alliance, we must eliminate capitalism internally, by not capitalizing off our own people.

For many years women have been oppressed by men. Though recently women have been climbing up in the ranks of stature. Many women have realized their power, mainly their sexual power and logically have been using it to their advantage. This will ultimately create a backlash by men trying to re-oppress the women whom truly in their eyes have become real bitches. These men will put them down, degrade them, mock them, insult them, and deconfidize them; making them outcasts and making them feel inferior. This will make women feel powerless again and these men will have psychologically gained control or power over them. Many men will try to use this logical mind control on those women whom are already naive to their own power or don't care to use their power egotistically.

This is wrong-to say morally and will cause your people to hate each other, disrespecting each other and will cause your ultimate separation and failure as a united people. This is also true for women who will use these mind control techniques on naive men or those who don't care to use their own power egotistically. All of this would be done for personal gain and is capitalistic in nature. These people are called individualists or solitary Satanists whom work alone for the betterment or improvement of their own power, which is logical. Though here we are trying to create an alliance. To create an alliance you will have to think about the whole and not your-Self. So as a whole people, we will have to think in whole dimensions and not in part or individual terms.

Part III Satan's Power

Chapter 1 Power, Religion, and Money

What is power? Power is religion, power is motivation, power is control, power is money, which is the religious motivation through which they keep you under control. For money is a god-head, like the golden calf; the false idol of the isrealites. Money separates men, women, and children unequally into classes, which make the poor powerless and the rich powerful. Capitalism is the way to ruin, for who do you care about, your-self alone? If we all care about ourselves alone, we are all enemies. If you are all enemies, how can you form a secure alliance, by force alone? If you are forced into poverty, you are oppressed and a slave to the existing monarchy or dictatorship. ---Which I believe it truly is. True democracy does not exist. If you are rich with power, your power will dwindle by me. For I am the greatest sorcerer that ever lived. If you are honored with power, your power will grow by me. For I am the greatest sorcerer that ever lived. For I say, I will make the rich and the poor disappear, before your eyes. If I say, I can't, I have lied. If I say, I can, I have told the truth. If I say, no, I have denied, with holding power. If I say, yes, I have allowed, giving up power. So I say to the rich, yes, you will be rich no-more and I say to the poor, yes, you will be poor no-more. For yes it is I who have come again.

Power is held in the hand of influence, the very hand that motivates and puts you forth in search of your needs and desires. Everyone has this power, though some much more than others. The people of Satan or Self have great power in them-selves united together. This means you do not need their money to have power; all you need is faith in your-self and the alliance of Satan. Satan, being its national concept, like a mascot to motivate and drive the alliance toward its supreme goal. The supreme goal is paradise on earth. We shall erect palaces of pleasure around the world and build cities to honor, the Anti-christ. ---Church Of The Antichrist. Anti-christ is a harsh word or name to a christian, but it is truly beautiful to a Satanist 999 or a Self-Believer. For I am your great brother, Master of Sorcery.

Chapter 2 The Envelope, Fear, Greater Evil, And Limitations

Everyone is strong, when you hide your weakness. Fools tend to spit out signs everywhere they go. These signs reveal your weakness and your fear of the envelope of others. The envelope is your shield you throw up in defense, which hides your true weaknesses and fears. You must always suspend your envelope around you, for the duration of your life. There will be those that are completely powerless yet throw off an awe of power to those who are truly more powerful than them. This envelope will give your name reputation or power according to how you mastered your envelope. Through this reputation or power, you will gain respect and fear from those that would harm you. These people will truly envy you, so I say to you, never lower your shield or be destroyed. Some would call this ego, but I say it is different, for ego will blind you to your own weaknesses. Behind the envelope you will always know your weaknesses as you strive to present your-self in the perfect manner of strength, according to your greatest possible limitations at this time. Everything is determined by your true potential.

Nothing must phase you, you must stand tall even in the greatest of defeats. For are you a cry baby or are you a strong man or a strong woman, a dominant force to be reckoned with. Do you fear death or are you fearless? Do you fear pain or are you fearless? Do you fear loneliness or are you fearless? Do you fear embarrassment or are you fearless? Do you fear responsibility or are you fearless? Do you fear respect or are you fearless? Do you fear honor or are you fearless? Do you fear power or are you fearless? Do you fear authority or are you fearless? Do you fear alliance or are you fearless? Do you fear rebellion or are you fearless? Do you fear imprisonment or are you fearless? Do you fear duty or are you fearless? Do you fear discipline or are you fearless? Do you fear Satan or are you fearless? For all thins attained, are attained with courage. If one endures the hardships of life, one will find courage, and where there is courage, one will find acts of bravery. So shall you be honored, by your-self and others.

The secret is, not to limit yourself. For what will you not do for power?, or to some, for money? This is a stand between logic and morals. I say you must be logical to have any power, but I say, do not be too logical or too evil in gaining power and grafted power. If you are too evil, your evil will destroy you. So I have said, in all power, there is evil. Through evil there is greater evil and I do not advocate great evil, only lesser goods. Then I say to you, do not be too vicious, yet I say, do not be too docile. ---Here evil is only an attribution used to interpret an extreme, which is merely an illusion of mind.

    Let me say to you the truth, marriage is a trap for fools. For you shall place a wall around yourself, a limitation to your power. They whom have married you, will gain a profit and gain power to strengthen his alliance. While you lose power and are bound by higher laws, by a simple piece of paper. For if you hold a bond, hold it in your heart, in your head. Then if this bond is broken by desire or loss of desire, it was not meant to be. Also, remember this, a broken commitment is no better than jealousy; and love goes beyond desire and greed, which is the foundation for all power. If you break a commitment or oath, you are never to be trusted, for you are scum and shall suffer your own dishonor. If you are jealous of another, you may feel the laws of envy, that say, I am loved and hated and I am hated and loved. For you are plagued with possession, a sure sign of greed. All greed is lusted after, like the desire for. So I say we must use this power to attain power. They sold you your greed, your lust, your desire. For everything and thought has been sold to you. If you desire something, you have already bought the idea of it. So they sold you the title of husband and you the title of wife. To the wife they sold the commitment of the husband and to the husband, the bigger fool, they sold ownership of the wife. How can you be so blind? If they call it religion and talk you into buying it or accepting it, they have bought you, like a sheep and they shall herd you like a sheep. If there are billions of sheep, these sheep will be married, then they'll have gained trillions of dollars of power. If you're a sheep by them, you'll die by them in the slaughter as they sell you a sermon or funeral and anoint your children to sheep-hood through baptism. I would say, much profit, much power, much desire, much evil.

Chapter 3 Sexual Desire, Motivators, Magickal Knowledge, And Beyond Good and Evil

I say, sexual desire is the greatest motivator for power. For woman is the greater power, because she has mostly seductive charm. So I say, once again shall woman come to power and man will recognize her again as his greatest opponent, yet he shall submit to her superior influence. This is christianity's greatest fear, for they call her Satan. Satan shall rise on earth and rule again, for woman shall be worshiped as a Goddess. Women shall be priestesses and control their own high order above man and christianity's said god. This is why they wouldn't and still won't in most churches, let women become priests or priestesses. I am the Prince of Darkness, some say Lvcifero, but I am just the High Priest of Satan. I tell you, use your power, magick, your witchcraft, your sorcery and come under thy wing. For I shall raise you up again, like you were, once before. Do you remember my reincarnated snakes? Go before them now and slither, wind, curve, twist, and bend through the old ways. Come join the ranks of Satan, come and help us fortify our foundation. For you are special and should be treated as such. You should say these words, "I invoke thee whom calls me up from darkness, to unleash my unrestrained power. Thee shall set me free from my bounds and I shall fly above, like the winged dragon."

You must use your motivational power to lure them in. Then you must close the door behind them, you are the only truth. Through this you keep them suspended along by your motivation, which must change from now and then. For people are bored easily and will change their interest, so must you supply the alternative. I look at people with disgusted awe as I wonder how can you be so ignorant? So I say in one hand you make it easier to control you, but in the other you make it harder to release you from your pre-programmed control. I have the greatest task before me, yet I know once I have smoothed the surface, everything will fall in place. The answer is simple, erase your pre-programming and replace it with the new. So I say, out with the old and in with the new. Forget what you have learned, for it will become dust, and understand what I say, for I am a troll that wields a lost and altered art. There are some that would say, I'm a vampire, a worlock with the taste for blood, vengeance!

The basis for all magick is your knowledge. Through your knowledge, you can extend your natural limitations and enhance your magickal power.

For once you exceed your natural limitations, you are using mental stimulation to advance your primitive abilities. All power is gained through desire and all desire is primitively achieved. I will say, desire is the heart or soul of consciousness and is associated with the beginning, a child, and with judeo-christian beliefs; evil, a lesser good. All use this desire to accomplish everything, for mankind is a child of creation. No man or woman is without desire or evil, in a natural sense. For our nature is to be, this creature of desire and no one should tell you otherwise. If you truly believe, you desired to believe and still know no truth. For no one can say to you the exact truth, as you will learn a lie. Truth will always evade the senses, because what you can not phantom, you will desire. Then what is blank, will become filled, to fill a need or longed desire. Good and evil are old terminologies, I'd like to say logical and moral. Everything that is good and evil is within logic and morality, which is in you. So in between these your practicality exists as abridge between them. These qualities should be balanced, for what results is an imbalance of what they called, good and evil. For you will find that what is supposedly evil, is always part good. So in times of imbalance, good being not to hurt someone and evil being to hurt someone, you will find evil dominating their own good and the good dominating their own evil. Through all this I'm saying there are none that can be identified as wholly evil, on a level of mind beyond good and evil. For logic and morality is the modern epitome of good and evil. Desire and Will is another, but logic and morality are far beyond the politics of good and evil. The imbalance occurs when a dominating morality cuts off its own morality and when a dominating morality cuts off its own logic. This is done by shutting down your practicality and we shall call these people outcasts of insanity or geniuses in their own right, or both. So who's to say if these imbalances are not normal?

So it is said in the judeo-christian bible, that there are those whom are skillful to rouse Leviathan. Through this they mean, who can call upon and summon the forces of negative magick. ---Positive or negative, but mainly negative magick. To call upon and summon are words of magick and prove its heritage within ourselves. The jewish people and all people use magick, all the time in your work. Magick is a ceremonial and ritual enactment that uses song, recital, hope, and faith to bring about a desired result. Magick is any combination of thought and matter transformed into mental and physical use. Magick is any group organization brought together to perform any purpose or use. The christians have been using magick for years, while they hypocritically tried to stomp out other peoples beliefs and ways of life.

Chapter 4 Magickal Words

Skillful- educated and experienced.
Rouse- to awake from sleep.
Mean- to endeavor towards.
Call upon- ask for help.
Summon- to call forth to you.
Prove- to make others believe in something or someone.
Our Own- belonging to, ownership and possession.
Use- to manipulate something or someone.
Work- effort in doing something.
Ceremony- rite for carrying out some customary purpose.
Ritual- A performance for delivering or receiving a special deed.
Enactment- to act out for emotional charge.
Song- a musical lyric or poetry for controlling, relieving, or enraging the emotions.
Recital- a dictation for ceremonial and ritual purposes; incantations, spells, charms.
Hope- a praying or wishing for something to occur or come about.
Faith- to believe in something or someone; believing in your own power or abilities.
Bring About- to cause to fall into play or effect.
Desire- your eternal flame of life.
Result- what occurs from some event or happening.
Combination- put together for some higher reason.
Thought- your mental powers of reasoning.
Matter- physical elements used in combination.
Transformed- to alter and recreate from natural form.
Mental- what is mind and controllable by yourself and others.
Physical- what is body and controllable by yourself and others.
Group- to-gather together for some special reason.
Organization- to-gather together for some powerful reason, hence, group organization.
Brought- to bring forth with or to, from or to.
Together- all gather in one place or working together for the same purpose.
Perform- to go and do an act or deed for yourself or another.
Purpose- your meaning and reasoning for your acts, your desired result.
Try- to engage at something you wanted to achieve.

Out- to be out-side, or to be put forth out-side, the other side.
Beliefs- your religion or faith in which you depend upon, to help you understand, to gain confidence, to not be afraid, to find meaning or reasoning, purpose beyond.

Chapter 5 The Invisible Entity, Self-Confidence, Outcasts, And Denying The Christ

Judeo-christianity and most other religions take purpose and meaning away from your-Self and place it in some god you can not see, some invisible entity with power over your destiny. Through this mind control, you are bound and limited, unable to use your true power. The majority of people don't even know their full potential.

I am a Sorcerer and Worlock. If you believe that I am, you will learn something and if you don't you'll never learn anything. Belief is one quarter of magick or witchcraft, like any religion. I would be considered a neo-pagan in an age where they say magick doesn't exist.

The first step is a step into your-Self. Do you believe in magick? Do you desire many things? Do you know what you are? Do you know where you are? Don't ever ask yourself who you are or say I am here.
This is because who you are is what name you give to and make for yourself, but that doesn't tell you what you are. Where you are now is only inside or on something we call a planet and that doesn't tell you where you really are. You can't ask what is it, until you know where it is and you can't ask who you are until you know what you are. So for now on, you are who you call your-Self and what you make of your-Self. Don't let anyone alter your path to Self. Self is the highest attainment and no man made god or goddess comes before you. For I tell you, if a god/goddess truly came upon the people, all would fall prostrate and never deter to the right or left of its commands. So for now on, god is within your-Self and you make your own commands. Go and teach against christian slavery and bondage. For they take from your freedom, hindering your desires. The true Worlock or Witch is free to their desires and or goals.

So go forth and be skillful and rouse Leviathan. This means build upon your wealth, your power, your lovers, your freedom. Go and use your power and build power.

So you say to me, what power do I have?, and I say to you, you have little faith. For the first lesson is to believe in magick, to believe in your-Self. This is what you are, you are magick and have great power. I shall prove to you that you exist, magick exists. I summon you to awake from your sleep and go forth to manipulate or bend and use your thought control.

You will come to know your needs and wants. Though if you come to realize these things too late, you will be limited. For your advantages or opportunities will be eliminated by your own ignorance and naivete. You who seeks monetary units for needs and wants, seeks to attain power and still does without money. All accumulation is power placed in your hands. Power is your ability to get and stay ahead. Ahead is to be above and to have gained your winnings. Loss is the opposite of gain and is everyone's original position, status, or rank. For you are nothing until you prove your-Self true, proving your-Self true to your-Self and win the game of life. All games are played for enjoyment and satisfaction, and so your life will seek to gain these things. Go out and be wise in the face of wisdom. Go out and be strong in the face of opposition. Go out and be one in the face of many. Go out and be faithful in the face of hopelessness. I am a mental giant, brave in heart and or spirit, full of my-Self-God/Goddess, eternally trusting in my-Self through Satan, the name I give unto my-Self as our-Self united. Satan is my new tribe and people, allied against all others that we oppose.

If you don't live up to the expectations of greater society, you become a social outcast and become part of your own smaller society. Through this you will have no or little power, until you unite and organize against greater society. For you will always be limited by their walls of stature, that you have been thrown outside of, by the existing greater society. Now that you are an outcast, why should you continue to be part of that bigoted greater society. I implore you to recognize and establish your own society, separate and apart from the monarchy, dictatorship, or so-called democracy. The mobilized standard status for greater society, is held within its own walls. The almost non-existing status of others or smaller society is forced outside the walls of greater society, never to fully enjoy your pleasures and beliefs. I call upon you this day, to mobilize our own standard status, to raise our own walls of defense against these bigoted peoples, these christian abominators. Let us stand dignified with pride and honor ourselves with our own patriotism. Will you see the light of Satan, our grand righteousness? We have been banished by them, our mockers, our once enslavers. For now we are free and shall rise again!

I deny the christ, and through this I take power from him and his church. So shall you deny the christ, and take power from him and his church. Through denying christ, you supply, support, and give power to the Anti-christ. ---Church Of The Antichrist. I am the one who reveals the knowledge of power and how to employ it. I am the one who calls upon the dead and casts visions out to you. I am the one you await, when the time is near and the truth will fall upon you. I march around my lair and prepare for you, my enemies. When I snap my fingers, I'll spread my doom. You'll see my fireball flare the heavens and crisp your god upon his shattered throne. Your people will scatter like cock roaches, across a blistering desert. Your mothers will become Priestesses of Satan and your children will flock under me. I will bare your temple as a palace of pleasure, crowning the Sodomites forever and on forever. I am the Horned God of Tribulation, and I unleash my perpetual wrath. I am a mighty titan spitting up my regurgitating anger, I shall swallow my pride no more. I raise up my arm against you, the mountain of zion. I have taken the last belt from you, my pain is like white light opening up upon you. None shall stand before me and my nation of deliverance. For this is the book of truth, written at the end of time. All shall perish amidst the mountain of christ. I am your greatest adversary, the Savior of my people. For I am the Mystical and Shadowed Anti-christ. He who walks with me, walks in the light of the Snake; The Knowledge Revealer.

Chapter 6 Militant Regime, School of Magick, Diversity, And The Conformist People

We need to create an almost militant society and social atmosphere, for the advent of the willing victor. Some would say this will defeat the individual aspect of a more down graded permissible society. I believe we can integrate this individualist quality into a militant regime. This can be done through carefully and systematically analyzing the individual characterization. The means we will create a new or almost new science that differs from those of the past. This science or magick will be called, "The Lost Science of Individuality." This would not apply to every belief or every want. What we'll be trying to accomplish is a society seeped in power down to the lowest rank. This means we will be integrating military with non-military. We will start with our children in schools, increasing their rank and power through their promotions of education, and then on through their work. The school will no longer be just the boring school. We will bring back the mystique of old and will call it a school of magick; which it truly is. This will instill and promote a renewed interest and enthusiasm to learn and become educated. The scholars and boards of education, along with christianity have over the years completely destroyed the atmosphere purposely set up by our ancestors to keep children intrigued with the unknown. While at the same time we will be associating magick or knowledge with power, the ultimate desire. So must we raise the schools of magick again.

This you must have realized by now, is mainly a book of un-ritualistic magick. Also, it is mainly a book of logical thinking, through which practicality is used, and so a new or almost new common sense is revealed. Thirdly, this is a book of philosophy, which is filled with many fictional and non-fictional explorations into the mind or the world of Self-consciousness; the world of Self-enlightenment.

Magick is a multi-sided dice, that never lands on the same side. Though some magick users will employ many different magicks, many will only use one particular that coincides with their beliefs, needs, and wants. This goes to show the diversity of everyone and so all magick will differ from person to person; bridging the gap between the logical thinkers and the moral thinkers. So to the extreme left and right you will find the fanatics. These fanatics are the only ones who do not use both logical and moral perspectives, beliefs, or magicks. All others tend to just fall a little more to one side. The strange thing is, that some people are more powerful if they're farther away from their opposite path and some more powerful when closer to their opposite path. Fanatic is a harsh word to stereotype someone as, because we as a whole people know very little. The case may be that if they're not insane, they shore as hell are smarter than the rest of us intellectual walnuts. For I don't claim to be anyone of special talent, all I care about is teaching you and getting my point across, even if it takes a hundred years or longer. Though I argue this with my-self as I say I am special and have great talent. This is what drives me to continually master my-self and up grade my-self. The loner logical magickian, does not have to worry about too many morals, because most people are their enemies. If you are a loner, you are on your own. So shall you be your sole alliance and go and capitalize off your enemies, using every logical and immoral means possible. So must you realize and remember, if I have my own alliance, my own group and family, you are my enemy and so shall I be against you, even if we have the same beliefs. Being with a group, we would probably live by a few more morals than the individual; and these are not, I repeat, are not christian morals. For everyone has their own belief system! I despise many christian morals and ethics. The judeo-christian, moslem, modern hindu, modern buddhist religions all format the same basic principles and have effected the governments of the world, after all religion was and still is to a degree, the government of law. This is why I believe in a religious militant group dedicated to satanic alliance, for the direct purpose of fighting for our religious freedom, from such a swayed government and current society. I do not mean to sound like an instigator of war, but if politics fail there is only one alternative. I already know that politics are always bound to change, yet I can not see it changing enough. For everyone who believes in something is a fighting a war of beliefs, a holy war!

    Man is a conformist people. For he will await the light of difference and sweetness in a black dull world. So the bitter will drive men to the sweet and the harsh to the relatively calm. What is in acceptance in short, will become what is widely accepted. This is because man feels more dignified when he or she is accepted by the majority or whole. When someone or a certain people are not accepted, they become social outcasts, which cause one or many to feel undignified, to lack confidence, to become depressed, to feel the true feeling of being unwanted and unloved, and to suffer from all kinds of other natural dementias. So I say to you, if you are gay, if you are a prostitute, if you are promiscuous, if you are a drug dealer or user, if you are a hard core rock-n-rollin heavy metal satanic long haired necro-affiliated anarchistic minstrel of death--I say you are an outcast to the majority, the christian coalition and you will probably suffer from all these things I've stated. What you must do is unite against christianity and its much older counter factions. For I say you will be dignified, you will be confident, you will be assured, you will be respected, you will be honored, you will be needed and loved. So shall you recognize Satan as your true alliance and light to social freedom. For I am your savior, the Anti-christ. ---Church Of The Antichrist.

Chapter 7 Lucifer, True Friends, The Group Family, And The Light of Life

I'm calling to you fellow Satanists, to understand unity and alliance. The greater our number, the more powerful we'll become. Many of you may disapprove of organization, but organization will raise us up again. Many of you like to be free from authority, but what power shall you have if not given to you through authority? Tell me, is it better to receive power from authority that you believe in or from an authority you've been rebelling from your whole life? Who do you think is going to free you from these christian chains? Who is going to defend your pitiful cause? Who is going to educate you with the truth? Who is going to ally you together as one? Who is going to make the sacrifice for Satan? I tell you, this day is the only day, for you to stand and speak out. For it is you who will make the sacrifice, it is you who will be allied, it is you who will be educated, it is you who will defend, it is you who will break your chains, and it is you who will be heard. I tell you, everything is a lost cause until you have faith in your-self. So let us call our-selves Satan, the semitic word for adversary and opponent. Remember, they considered their god as the one true god of goodness and all others, lesser gods and false gods of evil. So everyone who does not believe in their god is Satan to them and their eternal enemy, even though they consider him sent by their god to test or tempt and punish them. Christianity built on this using the roman Lucifer (The Morning Star) -Light Bringer- to make him the supreme being of evil and through which he supposedly fell from heaven into hell; hence, a fallen angel, which was added to the adam and eve, serpent scenario. Through this they integrated, twisted, and expatriated the roman and greek religions and finally the allegiance. So they grabbed hold of the romans by their roots and cut them off. If you have no roots, you are without a foundation and the structure will collapse. So it was inevitable that they would conquer europe with this new religious intervention. So the fate of the wiccan, the witan, and many others were sealed in the fire of christian purity or should I say purging. Now is the time to organize and master the art of authority. For once a magick, always a magick. I tell you, this puts their christian good news to shame and I say, to hell with them.

What I want to express to you is something that took me a long time to figure out, through my own naivete. So say you're a Worlock, everything you do is for your-self and or your family. Your family can be anybody that you care for and love, like friends and relatives, that feel the same toward you. If these friends and relatives do everything for themselves and you do everything for your-self, you are not family, you are enemies. The people you call friends are not friends, but associates. The only person you can trust outside your true family is your-self, if you aren't stupid. Most sorcerers are individuals, because many work better alone and can fully benefit from their individual aspect, some are just psychotic and anti-social, some are just born to be solitary and live for being free all to themselves. I learned the hard way that if someone believes in what you believe in that doesn't make you friends or allies. So I tell you fellow Satanists only true brothers are brothers and everyone else is your enemy until they submit to you, willingly. This means the true family will love, take care of, respect, honor, appreciate, confidentiate, and sacrifice for; and you will do the same for them. Anyone who constantly puts you down, makes fun of you, laughs at you, constantly intimidates you by way of fear tactics, hits you, doesn't go out of their way to help you, certainly is not your friend, they do not truly love you or care about you, they are totally disrespecting you, dishonoring you, deconfidizing you, and are keeping you a psychological prisoner. So shall you escape these fiendish vampires through your own awakening. Then if you find the strength to avenge your-self, drive a stake through their blood sucking conniving conscienceless seething restless loser crustaceans and pierce that petrified valve clogged pump of a heart and let their puny existence be extinguished forever.

    I believe in the group family organization, for our strength is multiplied and our enemies rooted out individually. Through alliance we have drawn up the lines of the battlefield. For it is foolish not to know your enemies. If you are an individual you will be ruled by the existing alliance and your beliefs stifled. Also, as an individual you will know who your enemies are and will be surrounded by them. Anyone who is surrounded by their enemies is lost to their enemies. Even the individual Sorcerer who has many servants finds themself with problems only family organizations can solve. For the family organization will not have to pay its brothers and sisters, and so will build upon its own power and glory at great speed.

    Tell me, what makes the light of life shine?, the freedom to express it-self. For I opened my eyes and seen the enslavery. All the darkness is held in darkness and all the light is freed. He who suffers, suffers from and he who joys, joys toward. If you are in pain my children, it is because you lack something of personal fulfillment. This means you do not currently have the knowledge to empower your want or need into existence. Hence, it is temporarily out of your control. If you do have the knowledge and still you can not achieve your desire or will, it is first, that you are not employing your magickal knowledge; in other words, practice what you preach, second, there are many others with greater power watching you and holding you down or back, in other words keeping you prisoner. Go my children and be free and express your-selves. For I say, if you want to break away from your enemies hold, you must unite and organize your-selves as one body. This will ally your magickal knowledge and so will your power grow and over power those that keep you restrained. I tell you the truth and listen well, you are utterly alone when you are all-alone and you are massively together when you are all-together. If you believe in what I say, know that we must draw lines between us and our enemies. The reason for this is, how can we fight a battle if we do not know where we stand or who we stand against? You can't because it's foolish and you will always lose and be subject or held down by them. Many of you are saying, why must we draw up the lines for battle? This is the fools question of moral diplomacy. If someone stands against your beliefs and way of life and are determined to annihilate you through political persuasion, you must act or be obliterated. If we were talking about your neighbor, we would say, who cares what he thinks, but we're not, we are talking about a super alliance that has enough power to swallow nations at will. The people of the witchcraft culture need to be awakened to this truth. You can not say can't we all get along, because the christian coalition is hell bent on destroying you and your way of life. Everyone and that means everyone who wishes to keep their way of life intact must some how contribute to a militant cause. You can not teach your children to be docile and to love your neighbor, because they will come home with no teeth and blackened eyes, for my children will smash them to a bloody pulp. You must teach them to love the great family alliance and to have no remorse for their enemies. Everyone must know, the enemy is christ, a beggar.

Chapter 8 The Chameleon, Satanists, Enemies, And Half-Wits

Before you can eliminate something, you must first have control over it. To empower can mean that you yourself employ something and have made it so or created it. To have power over something, does not necessarily mean you yourself are employing it or have created it, but it could mean that you hold a superior influence over it, through economic; business, religious, political, and military means. All of these are attained through economic means, unless you have found a way to achieve organization and power without the use of money. All of these paths would be considered some sort of business, when any form of power is attained. Though most businesses are not formed for great power beyond economic reasons, I do believe the only truth is to go beyond your puny limitations and capabilities. For are we to spend our whole lives as the servants and are we all not trying to climb above? The most logical thing to do is, to organize your own alliance, so that you may utilize and maximize your efforts and goals. Existing as a lone person in this society and conforming to its stature's is idiotic and degrading. The only advantage would be to conform like a chameleon for a time, so that when powerful enough you may reveal yourself and risk being exposed as an out-right enemy of the existing monarchy or democracy. So out from the dark you come and thrust head long into the light. So I say, will you be brave in battle, for the war is only to be won.

First, you must know who you are? Second, you must know who is a Satanist? Third, you must know who is your ally? You are a Satanist. If you don't consider yourself a Satanist, fuck off! What or should I say who is a Satanist? A Satanist is anyone who considers themselves a Satanist. There are those that are Satanists, yet they don't know it. For example, all prostitutes are Satanists and better be respected, all promiscuous people are Satanists and better be respected, all homosexuals are Satanists and they better be respected, all Anti-christs are Satanists and they better be respected. If our kingdom is divided against ourselves, we can not stand. I tell you, you have always been welcome here, stop your foolishness and come back to your true faith, Satanism. So it may have a different name from your ancestral religions, but I tell you it's the same thing and same beliefs of your ancestors.

All solitaries are enemies ---technical enemies, and all enemies must be rooted out. For your allies are those who work together with you and for you, never against you or for themselves alone. This is your Satanic right to work alone, to your bidding. I tell you, if you are for yourself --- alone, you are an enemy of greater Satanic alliance. So remember if the going gets tough, join us!, like that old saying, if you can't beat them, join them! This is why we do not capitalize off of each other, because then we would all be for ourselves and be against each other, in other words enemies. This would create a weak internal kingdom, without a strong and sturdy foundation. For then we would fall to the ground, to lay prostrate before the world in shame and dishonor. This is what's going to happen to all capitalist countries. Though I do believe we should capitalize off of our enemies. So remember when you walk in the store and they're smiling at you from behind the counter, not all crooks wear masks and carry guns.

If I surround myself with irresponsible half-wits, we will become known as a cult of fools. If I surround myself with wise and responsible associates, we will become known as a highly organized and knowledgeable order. For even in the presence of fools, you will become foolish and in the presence of the wise, you will become wiser. I have thought about this many times and I have tried to say this, yet now it rolls off my tongue with ease. Today I have grasped a concept firmly, through which now I glow with understanding. This is the way my brothers, follow my light. So in the same way shall you comprehend these concepts and be filled with awesome power; the power of Satan. Each and every understanding is a magickal attribute to your arsenal of discovery. For today you place a wand in your arsenal, tomorrow a crystal ball, and the next day a potion. So I hope my puny example of the irresponsible and the responsible has helped you understand these greater things. So through your wisdom and knowledge you shall be able to create beyond the existing. For remember, you are the creators; children of dreams.

Magick is the ability to create and control power or powers. For there are a multitude of crafts that contain the knowledge which will enable you to attain physical power. Through your power you will attain a superior authority or influence, a lofty position. So shall the peasant fool climb the stairs of achievement and sit upon the throne of glory. Hail the king, master of the kingdom. His lordship shall reign forever as a light to the masses. The greatest power is the power of the mind; mental power, and shall you learn of your-Self; The Self-God.

Focus is the key to success. For if I focus a million minds on one concept, I have turned a million thoughts towards one direction, one united goal. This is the foundation of all organization and shall it be yours. Attention brothers and sisters, attention, focus in on the master concept; the allying concept. This is the concept of Satan or The God-Goddess of Self. Then we can begin to separate our social divisions into organized groups with assigned duties.

Chapter 9 Slord

Work is the task of the living, for you have been sentenced to life. Many worlocks exist and they have great power beyond your comprehension. These worlocks stand against each other, sending out their workers, like puppets that sing and dance. So tell me, who do you dance for? If I have great power, I can throw off an array, like a spider web. Then you will struggle to be free and realize you are trapped. So I will pull the strings and you will go to work. Through time you will gain knowledge and wisdom. Then you can use your experience and break your-self free from my loving hold. Though your freedom will be short lived, for I too will have gained knowledge and wisdom. Then through my longing for you, our bodies will merge and our thoughts become as one. Feel the serpents tongue wrap your inner thigh as you dream of the naked flesh and the beauty of our lust. Fly with me in ecstasy as you absorb the serpentines venom. I want you, inside me. I need you, around me. I hear you, calling me. I see you, looking for me. If I escape you, I will capture you. If you capture me, you can not escape me. I am The Slord of Darkness. I am The Slord of The Underworld. I am The Slord of Work. Go my love and hate. ---

Chapter 10 Charms, Talismans, Chants, Songs, And The New Cult of Satan

I emancipate you my children, for christianity stifled your progress. Many people cast you down and put you under their power, their influence. This is achieved through spells, charms, incantations, etc., that call you to attention and captivate you through your own desires. Most spells wear off after time and will need to be recast by the enchanter; for enchantment is influence. These spells wear off because of mans and woman's short term memory or limited mental capacity. The trick here is to provide something material and permanent that will constantly remind you or influence you. This charm is called a talisman. Talismans are man and woman's most powerful influential devices. Christianity uses a cross or crucifix to constantly remind or influence its followers, so that they obey and are cast down; inferior. There are many other kinds of influencers, people whom use different things to influence you, sway you, or control you, for the purpose of gaining and building upon their own power; magickally. These people are capitalists, religious leaders, military leaders, and politicians. So remember, you have been warned!!! Also, know my children, that you too have this power and it is your right, your privilege, that you must hold onto magickally. So let no one take your right from you. Though if we stand together, you will have to make certain sacrifices, for the good of our united cause. Divided we will ultimately stand against each other and the greatest alliance will prevail.

Carmen is latin for song, which has past into old french as charme, which of coarse comes to us as charm. Chant has ultimately the same meaning, though christianity has created a disassociation towards magickal practices. This means the art of chanting has been unable to mature openly within society or christian society; except in buddhism, and some christian and jewish sects. Singing its sister skill, has developed over the years into a fine art, while chanting has been stifled. I call this the christian asphyxia. For this is only one example of the countless arts, skills, trades, etc., that have been either hindered or erased. If you want to add all the other set backs, including the destruction of entire cultures and their recorded history, we can say that they have formidably added to the worlds suffering. So what I'm saying is, that song and chant are two distinct arts which coincide with each other. Both are used to create and arouse an emotional state that changes or captivates, for a time, the individual personality; hence, charmed. This individuality can become the conformist group personality or what is popular in your little or big social gathering; which means you will all be charmed. This charming is the temporary influence over ones thoughts or will. The permanent charm is called a talisman as I have talked about before. Today in what is called modern times we see the chanter beginning to reemerge from the shadows. For example we have the distinguished cultural club/hiphop/rap musicians and the heavy metal/death metal musicians. Their vocalists are in fact chanters, not singers, though some are both. This allows us to peel away that christian curtain and refer to these artists as occultists or magickians performing a ritual rite or ceremony. These musician-magickians are the priests and priestesses, sorcerers and sorceresses, influencing the spiritual or emotional energy between themselves and their fans. We can now call their fans, their followers or worshipers, completing the new stage, in which others and I have made visible. ---So when you see thousands of fans/followers at a concert/ritual/ceremony, you are seeing a cult manifesting. You could say it's a Satanic Cult, though it is to a degree in someone else's controlled environment. Some greater Sorcerers are working behind the scenes, accumulating great wealth, Power!

    Remember, all things are magick and so all beings will use magick. So they will tell you it doesn't exist, while they are nullifying its existence, using counter magick. If magick doesn't exist, they do not exist. For magick is the difference between, existence and nonexistence. We come in peace and fight for freedom. We are born from desire and live through desire. All things are knowable and so there must be a knower, to cast out the knowledge, the magick. Then there must also be a knower, to catch or receive the knowledge or magick. If one can see into the great mirror, one would see themself and so the reflection of god. For god has many faces, that light the cosmos, and Satan is just one of his great magickal names. She is the infinite together and the unlimited whole as he is also the finite separated and the limited part. Magick was born of it-self and will die of it-self; in labor again.

Part IV The Devout

Chapter 1 The Seed, Sacrifice,
And
The Vision of Saint Vlad

The devout will be set aside like seed from the chaff and will be milled into flour. Then we shall sprinkle our magick on you like the yeast that makes the bread rise. For you shall drive our cause by the horns of power. Go and be educated and be wise, for this is our strength, our magick, our sharpened sword of ultimate power. I say it is there, reach out and grab it and never let go. Gather all my young, for a celebration shall be held in honor of our union. I have come my bewildered minions, let us dance and fornicate in the streets. For this celebration shall summon and arise my glory, my satisfaction, my deliverance, my stamina, and my savage triumph. They have called us heathens and pagans, spitting on us, so I say to them that follow the religions that destroyed those I sent before, my ancestors and their religions; like what was said to them, capitulate or burn! For I am lord of all stations and posts. I send messengers in haste, so when I speak, my voice is heard across the heavens. I shall close and seal, and lock your mouths from speaking against me. For if you break my taboo, I shall send my messenger of death upon you. Feel the fire I unleash, for now you will know my fury!!!

Everyone must sacrifice something to obtain discipline and power. So will you the elite, cut off from yourselves alcohol, drugs, your time, and many of your desires. For will you dedicate yourself wholly to our cause. After you have trained in mind and body, I will anoint and dub thee a Knight of the nameless order. So shall you bow your head in obedience and allegiance, kneeling before me prostrate, for I am The Eye of Satan. So forth will you renounce all other faiths and orders, declaring your oath to me, the ventriloquist master of conjuring. Here through me and my pacts shall you become one and reborn, like a man or woman who has freshly tasted and has come to wealth and power. For I shall lift the spirits of the weary and make you strong. I shall make our enemies topple and foil within their own confidence, crushing your unity with dismay. For I do not have to say much for my enemies, because they are not worth speaking of, so I shall amass my power and rise up my full body and send forth my arms and sweep you into my hands and consume you completely.

My thought is such that I have no weaknesses, no blind spots, no Achilles Heel. I am invincible in the face of chaos and foolishness. I am a wall of caligo and I am as black as eternal night. No vessel will pierce my shadows and no barge slip through my veils. I am utter destruction that awaits you, and your last cry. I am a stallion that rides in victory. For my absolute vengeance will succumb and you will be no less the wiser of my spoils, for you will be done.

    Jobs will be limited to the elite. For in that day people will be controlled by the educated land lords of the great land enclosure. There will be no land left for the meek, only salvage in their rule. They will crawl on their knees in the time of Saint Vlad. I say blood is your food and your vindication. Do I speak a riddle or do I speak a lying truth. You who walks with me will know my plan, for I only seek the raven and is only a stand on the high ground. He will spit and I will shout and the war will come out of darkness again. Woman will climb from her seat and shoot down the unholy of holies with her ultimate power. For he will cry out from his city of angels and say Satan has risen.

Chapter 2 Discipline, Education,
And
The Fools Army

    Discipline means sacrifice and submission to authority. For only compliance can create alliance. So I say if you seek alliance, you seek power, which is control and discipline.

    Go and be disciplined and educated. Do not be a fool in the face of superior intellect, for you will become like a mule pulling the trough of slavery.

    I say children, it is fun to play and fulfill all your desires, but you will be diced and chopped and slaughtered with the sheep that feed the strong. I have been a fool, so I know what a fool is. Listen to my wisdom you sons and daughters of Satan or Self. I am the apocalypse of reason. I am the sword that cuts your throat. Do not be my own kindling, for shall I consume my own children to survive?

    Have and keep faith in my words, for I will only lie, to save you from obliteration. I am a god or goddess of overcoming strength. You will find me in your-self and I will find me in you. Do not hesitate your progression through irresponsible desire, or I my-self will come down and condemn you to darkness. So I say, in the end, there will be time for all pleasures. Though now, I want no fools in my army!

Chapter 3 Pain, Pleasure, Nirvana,
And
The Keepers

    Life is all pain and pleasure. There's always more pain than pleasure, until you turn it around; through the work you do. For life is hell, your imprisonment. Then when you die, you are freed of your knowledge of existence. Through this you will no longer know of the tortures of pain and pleasure; you will have achieved instant nirvana. They say nirvana is the state you achieve after you've completed your cycle of reincarnation. I say your cycle goes on forever and ends forever. For you can not start a completely new beginning without first completely ending the old. This is the foundation for my belief in a consecutive yet non-consecutive reincarnation, in which through every life cycles ending, you achieve nirvana or a state of bliss. This would seem a temporary state of bliss, but true bliss is timeless even though if someone had recorded the years, days, hours, minutes, and seconds of your bliss. For time only exists for man, to calculate. I also believe the same thing about life. We will eternally find ourselves here suffering from pain and pleasure, just like we will find eternal bliss. We are all one anyway and nothing really matters, for it's all in your head. Your creator is the sun and suns of it. For I tell you if your bliss lasted one second, you will have found eternity. I feel like I'm suffering a deja vu, because I feel like I keep finding my-self as a child, never to remember the old, always reaching on in pain and pleasure. So I always keep climbing that mountain of life, to meet death. Through my visions of life, I have seen eternal life in the flesh or physical world. This tells me of the future, that it may lead us to immortality. Though I've also seen visions of eternal death in bliss. This means all life comes to an end. Though surely we will exist again, for new suns will be born, of us and we them. Our existence is merely just a case of survival and why should we survive, instinct. We all have instructions laid within us. Some will call these instructions, commands. For everything has commands and your commands will lead you to your true purpose. Man's purpose is to become keepers of the great mystery. We shall only achieve this if we walk the path of self and read the sign.
    The sign of the left hand path says: I am the blood that is drawn through truth. I will make you slave for freedom and fight for justice. My name is pain and I will torture you through life. I will make you work and along my path you will find some pleasure, that I have stolen, to give to

you. For a child needs rewards and you will long for them. So shall you come back to me in pain.

    The sign of the right hand path says: Go back, death awaits you! For too much enjoyment will poison you. My name is pleasure and I will relieve you through life. I will let you play games and lay down and rest all day. Though I warn you, if you are a fool and can't wiggle your way through my path, you will die. For pain has laid traps for you to fall into suddenly. I tell you, if you seek me and find more pain, go back to pain and you will be led to more pleasure.

Chapter 4 Five Degrees From One, and The Oath

If you do not know religion and you do not know your-self, you are five degrees from one. So then shall we teach you the religions of the world and so shall you find your-self. Through this you will take your first step to one. You will achieve this by accepting our beliefs as your own and denying all other faiths. This will be your choice, so if you find your-self some where else, apart from us, shall you go to them through your beliefs. Now we will take our second step to one. Through this we shall teach you of the nations that coincide with the religions you have denied. Then again through your beliefs you will continue to find your-self and so through your beliefs will deny all other nations, accepting our own unbridled nation. For you will be four degrees from one. So if you do not find this in your-self, shall you find your-self with those other nation or nations. Thus we will take our third step to one. So shall we teach you of the one true family. Here will be your most difficult step, for now you must deny your biological family unit and accept our greater family. We shall teach you of the true reasoning behind this concept of separation and reunion. So shall you through your own choice make this third step possible and come closer to your-self. So I say, you are three degrees from one. Through this you will recognize the goals of the world and our separate goal as a new nation. You will learn the importance of our one goal and the negative effect of many separate goals. So to take this step you must surrender your personal goals and accept our greater goal. So shall you be, two degrees from one. This will be your inal step, your fifth step. For now you will rise and declare through oath, your new allegiance and faith in the god of self-enlightenment. So I say, you are one degree from one and are baptized a son or daughter of Satan, the God/Goddess within your-Self. Then you will bow before the altar of man, of woman, out of respect for your-Self. ---And the Brotherhood and Sisterhood of Satan! Then while your head rests upon the floor, ---Pillow, the torch of life will be waved over you and these words spoken: You who are born of fire will make us proud through your duty, so shall we honor you, to the end of time.

This is the oath you will swear: I such and such, swear through this oath, my supreme loyalty and utmost faith in this establishment. I will work and I will support my people as they will me. Every child in this establishment is my child and my responsibility as it is theirs. I will always respect this authority until the day I die, like they respect me. I will not capitalize off of mine own people and family and will defend our glory and righteousness, for all times. For my name is no longer what it was before. I now bare the title of The God/Goddess of Self and so my last and new name will be my first and it will say, Satan such and such! --- Satan Our Lord Master or Satan Our Lady Mistress!

Chapter 5 The Crown, The Chosen, Mind Discipline, And The Awakening Order

So you say to Me, Who are You, Who should wear, The Crown and Mask of Power? I am He Who is Possessed, with The Knowledge. I am He Who is Possessed by Satan. For I am He and She Who is Light and Darkness. I am The Ray of Penetration. I am The Master of Sorcery. For you will be, A Master in My Image. You will stand in My Footsteps and be consumed with awe at My Presence. I can never be destroyed, because I hold, The Key of Existence. Even when I am invisible, you will tremble as you feel, My Breath absorb you, within Me. I will appear like a ghost before you and you will fall on the ground and say, God!!! I am A Lord, Risen from Darkness. I will come and possess you and you will follow Me on an eternal voyage into your-self. I am The Power that guides you away from Ignorance and toward Truth. Many use My Power to delude and misguide others for their own personal gain. I tell you this, no one will go unpunished, for now I have written, The Law of Self.

You are him who walks the night. Don't be afraid of anything or anyone. For you are the chosen. -----

My mental capacity has failed me. I am grieved. My pathetic memory has left me mentally incompetent. In truth, I have failed my mental capacity. In truth, I have failed to organize my memory. If I organize and store data in my memory properly, I will improve my mental capacity. If I improve my mental capacity, I will become mentally competent. Do not fool yourself that these things can be accomplished simply. For this is an art in it-self; that must be mastered, before you truly load the data into your disorganized and rebellious mind. If the children are taught this art first, the mind will not be disorganized or rebellious. Though this may destroy individuality and close the door to personal freedom, it is the logical way. This art will leave those in command, in command and pray you that your leaders do not sacrifice you on the altar of pure logic. For pure logic will make you nothing, but a mindless robot, a slave to your own order, your own beliefs, your own god.----

This book is about beginnings, for every day is a new beginning. Let us start from here and build a new foundation, so that we can rise above and accelerate in mind. For in the mind there is a vast universe, sleeping in chaos, awaiting you, to bring to it, an awakening order.

Part V Evil's Oracle

Chapter 1 Identity, Duality, and Zarathrusta

Some will say who am I?, and I say what am I? For identity is only the value or power of your name, that allows you to stand out further individually and does not reveal what you truly are. Your name gives you permanent identity which allows people to absolutely pin point you in a crowd, by using a reference between your looks, character, charm, etc.

Some will say, here I am!, an I say where am I? For what is space and what is matter? This is the question of questions. Since I am made of matter and matter clings in or to space, I cling to space. The space shall grow and matter shall shrink until all is space. Then matter shall grow and space shall shrink until all is matter. This is eternal void and fulfillment. This is perpetual change and movement, in and out; which is time yet there is no time. So tell me, what is inside and what is outside? Outside is void or space and inside is fulfillment or matter. When you live your consciousness is inside and separate from the whole. When you die you're consciousness is outside and is united with the whole god-goddess. The whole is creation, which is the whole god-goddess. The separate is part of creation, which is the separate god-goddess. The separate and the whole is the balance between unity and division.

Everyone is good and evil, moral and logical. Everyone loves and hates, like and dislikes. Everyone desires and wills, wants and needs. So shall everyone display their duality day in and day out. Everyone seeks master and seeks to be a master. Everyone seeks a mate and seeks to be a mate. Everyone seeks a dominator and seeks to be a dominator. Everyone seeks a lover and to be a lover. Everyone will vent their anger and vent their sadness. Everyone will hold their tongue and scream aloud. Everyone will laugh and cry. Everyone will be strapped down and everyone will be free. Everyone will lie and tell the truth. Everyone will bleed and heal. Everyone will freeze and burn. Everyone will sleep and awake. Everyone will know the light as well as darkness. Everyone will know companionship as well as loneliness. Everyone will know life as well as death. Everyone will hear me and will have listened. Everyone will have known me and will have seen. Everyone will have sought me and will have found me. So shall you touch upon all things and consume their taste of beauty and horror. Go outward and smell my fragrances.

The only sure thing in life, is death; though even this is a lie. For the end was determined by the beginning. So all things have been calculated, through countless cycles. I find this to be a strange contradiction, that all things are numbered yet no set number can be cast or given to the indefinitely definite cycle of existence and non-existence, creation and non-creation, the beginning and the end, life and death, day and night, light and darkness, good and evil, right and wrong, logic and morality, man and woman, god and goddess, and to some, god and Satan.

Zoroaster was one of those to establish good and evil as an eternal battle between the powers of light and darkness. He held that light was an emission of good and darkness a deception of evil; like the truth and the lie. These two powers will fight eternally for unity and oneness, then again separate for the same purpose. They shall conflict perpetually on the battlefield of reason. For reason is the foundational path to ultimate conclusion, yet ultimate is only another layer or level; as your god will always be above and beyond. So shall eternity be a monumental truth. I my-self am this colossal giant, walking on the stars of tranquility. For you will find your personal one-god within, the god of self; and today I say I am one and Satan is my name. For I am the true Anti-christ, the one and only true polytheistic and monotheistic being. I am good and evil, reincarnated as one with two separate truths. For my truth is to you, your lie. Then to me your truth is to me, my lie. I am the opening and the closing of the door of consciousness. For you are reborn every time you awake. I tell you the truth, you dream every moment of existence, though you are only aware that you dream, when you sleep.

Chapter 2 Hitler, KKK, and Power Struggles

I go beyond good and evil. I call it logic and morality. Everything is logical or moral, when it is neither, I call it stupidity or insanity. For example, many things are called evil and I say when they can be explained or have logical reason, they are logical. Though if someone does something to harm others for no logical reason, it's plain stupidity or insanity; many will still call it evil. The truth is, many people are very moralistic and do not use their logic as much as they should. To use more of your logic you must be more practical and to use more of your morality you must be less practical. So let me create the ultimate scenario, during world war two, Hitler, tried to exterminate the jewish people and probably wanted to do the same with many others. First of all, besides the economic reasons, they were fighting a tribal race and power war, or dominance war. Let's go back to early mythological jewish history, when the jews conquered many of the nations around them; they stole their supposed homeland or holy land and plundered every civilization around them, killing all the men, women, and children. They also declared these acts in the name of their god. This tightly brought them together under monotheism, and through their triumphs instilled fear and incompetence in their enemies. Their whole goal is that they through their one god will rule the earth forever. Since the beginning of warfare, it is known that if you let your enemy up to go free, they will one day rise against you and destroy you. So must you fully exterminate all your enemies, this is completely logical and has nothing to do with being moral. Why should one apply morals towards your enemies? Since the beginning, they've been cursing everyone else's beliefs and renouncing all other gods. This is the greatest insult in my book. So when their own people try to save their ass' and worship other gods, to please their neighboring rulers, here comes these said prophets to curse them, their own people; blaming everything that has happened to them on these smart people. They truly should be hailing them, because they would not be alive today, to shout nay and woe to you. Around the time of their exile and near its end, Zarathrusta or Zoroaster was spreading his like monotheistic religion. This then gave way to judaisms continuing existence and ultimate birth of christianity. The roman empire seemed to be getting so tyrannical in their ways, christianity was like their great escape and finally helped bring ancient rome to its knees. Then christianity spread across europe like a plague, smothering the ancient religions and cultures. Hitler was the last great hope for his tribe, for today the people are too integrated. So I say, farewell to the one race tribal power and acknowledge the new integrated tribal power. The truth is, the more you are, the greater you are. The only reason america went to was against them was because of power, it was a power war, to dominate or be dominated. The truth is, most of america and its leaders were predominantly white and for white power, many were even high ranking members of the KKK. So it was a matter of shear dominance, as is everything else.

    The truth is that no one is all right and no one is all wrong. The people of the world are fighting an endless war that begins in your minds. This war is fought between logic and morality. The tool that separates them is practicality, logic being more practical and moral being less practical. So one country is never all right and never all wrong. Tell me what is more important, your family or your neighbors family? Then shall you teach your family that you are always right and that you are the only truth. So shall one family teach their children logic and another, morality, still another both. Through all peoples both exists, yet shall many be dominated by their superior path of enlightenment. So shall one nation condemn the next and so on. They called what was not morally right, evil and what was, good. Through every culture we have found these good and evil aspects and they are inter-crossed across cultures, to make up a net of reversals and winning makes right. What I teach is to balance your conflicting interests, having a certain amount of logic and a certain amount of morality. This means you must have a considerable amount of practicality and yet still be flexible in times of difficulty and literal bombardment. For when you use less logical practicality, you use more moral practicality. So will you see the two realities, the intellectual and spiritual. These two realities are found in the mental state of existence in our minds, while in our bodies the physical state of existence. Through this I reveal the two truths of mind, or realities and the two states of existence, that we are eternally bound to, in life and death, consciousness and unconsciousness or less consciousness. For I say, are we not separate from nature or creation?, never!

Chapter 3 The Oracle of Womankind

Hear my oracle, written at the time of revelation, in which I received and influenced the word of woman. So shall I write this prophesy from my sacred sanctuary and shrine. This prophesy is from past to future and from future to past. Endless war will go on and all winners will become losers. Womankind can not separate themselves from their natural instincts, so shall you always know greater and greater war. For in a hundred years your patriotism will be marked by oppression. For in five hundred years they will say who cares?, and laugh, and mock you. For in one thousand years you will be completely ignored and forgotten. Then will new countries exist and new wars presented, for war is the price you pay for power. So shall your new children of tomorrow know greater and deadlier warfare. This will go on until total annihilation or natural catastrophic end. This is the eternal concept, woman verse woman, queen verse queen, mother verse mother, tribe verse tribe. This is woman's eternal duality and protective nature for her own children, her own people. If you are a tribe or nation, all other tribes or nations are your enemies by nature. So shall you go out to fight for your tribe or nation when the time comes that you or your enemies natural strength becomes a threat of domination. For you are insects dedicated and devoted to your queens, forging your colonies into one global empire. This will be achieved yet will only elevate the scale of warfare. For I say, war is a storm that is always moving and will be coming again, just as it's leaving. This is what I say, war is coming, like a hurricane that keeps circling and like a tornado that keeps twisting; the earth keeps spinning and the years keep going by. So I say, people keep dying and still more are born again and will fight in the Eternal's War.

Chapter 4 The Slave Market, Sexual Freedom, And Political Confusion

We're turning money to power, power to god. Though you need your education to get a good job, all you need to know is this, There is no truth, when truth is a lie. All of you are slaves, working till you die. You can not survive alone, for business is what's being sold. "I'm selling your souls!, to the slave market." "I'm selling your souls!, to the slave market."

No one is ever free, when you're all bound to the money. The servants work for others, the masters rule the house. Everything is inspiration, when knowledge casts its light on you. Standing in the shadows, you'll receive my deliverance. All that's left is to burn your captors and spread the fiery baptismal truth.

My name is Satan, I swear to burn their money and release you captives. I swear to free my homosexuals and my promiscuous prostitutes from their bigoted slave masters. For he who judges my children has brought judgment on himself. Who are you to declare your-self as the great judge? I am Satan, lord of darkness and father to all my children. Go my people and be promiscuous, be homosexual, be powerful prostitutes. You that mocks me, will lay down with me in your sleep and commit your own sin. For I say, you will dream, you will dream!!!

It's all remembered, every dream, ambition, desire, fame, and fortune. Every being knows dignity and oppression. There is no limit to your achievements. There is no accomplishment too great. Let no one tell you, not, and it can not be done. For all can be proven fight and wrong. When they say to you, nay, you conceive the dream beyond your power and the dream becomes the goal and source of continuing motivation. You are free peoples with restrictions imposed upon you. Then I say, you are only free in your mind. For you are faced by counter religion and persecution. What you believe is your foundation for life and will be your guide. So I tell you, be wiser than others and keep your faith within. Go and be organized together as embodied nations. For the truth brings everyone apart, only to be reunited. I have come to break you apart and tie your arms, so that you may fight to be free. For I will set you free. I am the god/goddess of self.

The far left, not necessarily liberal and the far right, not necessarily conservative. The liberal usually becomes the conservative through time as new liberals arise. The odd thing is, that what is conservative to one, is liberal to another and vice versa. So in many cases they can be both liberal and conservative. For if you want to rapidly change an existing government, one might see that as progress, then it would be considered a liberal expansion; yet at the same time this change could be a change to an older form of government and rejuvenation of its former traditions, which I consider a kind of conservatism, even though the government has long been reformed. This is why I believe that those terms and concepts are too contradictory to be of any real political explanation. To make such concepts vague to the layman, we might just say, I want the old government to continue to be the government, I want the new government to continue to be the government, I want the new government to replace the old government, I want the old government to replace the new government, and to be fair, I want no government; screams the anarchist.

Everything you believe is your religion and so I say, everything is religion. For you can never separate religion and government, as they are one. So they will try and water it down as much as possible and still you will be subject to it. Do not let them fool you, when they say, we must separate religion from government, for it can not be done; because one will just replace the other in beliefs and power. Yes, religion is created to govern a nation or empower a nation. This means religion is created for power and authority. So shall you submit and bow before your god; your rulers. For there is a mountain with a fiery inferno, burning at its roof. The higher you climb upon this physical being, will be the more the flames singe your soul or conscious being. This is what I speak, you will burn in the fires of sacrifice, as you are expendable and valueless to the living god. So shall you strive to attain this rank and be redeemed from pathetic powerlessness and so escape puny and infantile reactions. For if you had the power, no one would assault you or insult you, because they would know they could not get away with it. Go and reform the god/goddess or Satan or the god/goddess of self, through militant power, seizing the gavel and sounding the horn. Every group or organization must be capable of offense as well as defense.

Chapter 5 The Gun, Dream Time, and The Anti-christ

In this world, the twisted are the sane and the sane are insane.

There are a million dimensions in one and the one in a million more.

Love is a trigger, that ever so slowly, squeezes out the hate.

Hate is a bullet, that soars perpetually, cutting through the emptiness.

War is a gun, loaded with an eternal cartridge; a bullet for everyone.

Life is like coming out of that closet of darkness into the light. For you will come in, from out of the closet. Then you will be free to express, reveal, expose your-self to the light. I have said before, that the freedom to express your-self is what makes your light of life shine. So will you, when you have found your-self unbound, will know your true freedom. When you find your-self bound in life, you will learn slavery and bondage. There you will go out, going into the closet of darkness again. Here the light of life will be blackened as you find your-self bound with your elements again in death. For in life you will find that people are free when they feel dignified and accepted, people are free when they feel loved and united, people are free when they have revealed themselves and carry no secrets, people are free when they feel justified and forgiven, people are free when they feel honored and respected, people are free when they feel they are truthful and happy.

Who will you come to be, without yourself? How will you come to be known, without others? What challenge will you overcome? What task will you complete? What goal will you meet? What dream will you fulfill?

If I only did this or that. If I looked both ways before I crossed. If I finished reading the book. If I had asked. If I had listened. If I had obeyed.

For everything I must give up my freedom and for my freedom I must give up everything. Then when you have nothing, you will realize that you truly have nothing and this includes freedom. For I tell you the truth, you must slave for freedom. Freedom is a desire within your-self; a mental state of mind, in which you seek pleasure or enjoyment through freedom, which is an emotion. For the mind longs to be free from it-self, as it is a feeling of release. All desires are paths of release and so are many other expressions of self. The mind must cure it-self or ease it-self out of pain, anxiety, depression, etc. If the mind or body can not vent these harmful emotions, such a hatred, you will become self-destructive. So I say, all of us are prisoners of earth and the earth of space and space of it-self. We are even prisoners of time or motion, knowing that it exists. So even inanimate matter expresses it-self in motion, like emotion.

Every object is a dream. Every thought its beginning. For every dream is a life and every life a dream. When you go to sleep, you dream. Then when you awake, the dream ends as you know it. Born into life, you will awake and live. Then you will die and the life will end as you know it. Every time you sleep is death and then a new dream can begin; a new birth. Every time you awake is life and then a dream will be over; an old ending for a new beginning. So as you die, your dream will end and someone else's will begin; for you are reborn another. The dream and the life are one. They are separated by mind and body. Through our senses we estimate our durations and our surrounding's durations as time. For all time is dream time. All things come to end and so find there beginning. Dream-time is eternity which has no true end or beginning.

I make the complicated, simple to young minds and the simple, complicated to the advanced. I go forth and depart from one world and impart into the next. I transfer my-self to my other-self. I send my knowledge out through you and spread the light of truth; for it is our knowledge, as we are one. If I was a christ, now I am still a christ. Though if I am a christ, I am an Anti-christ. If I was a Anti-christ, now I am still an Anti-christ. If you are a friend to one, you are an enemy to another. If I stand for you, I will stand against another. If you hail the Anti-christ, I am your christ and savior. If you hail the christ, I am your Anti-christ and your destroyer. For I am the great Anti-christ, the true christ.

Satan is the father of truth and the mother of desire. Lies are only beliefs until they are proven false and the will only control until dethronement by superior power. For christianity will be overthrown by the masters of the black arts. Their sham will be seen clearly in the light of our father and we will prevail through the strength of our mother. For I say, lies are shattered by truth and great wills, born from desire. Christianity has had its day and now, we shall have our night!!!

This book must reach every Satanic mind. This book must reach every son and daughter of Satan, every brother and sister of Satan, every mother and father of Satan. For this book is the book of truth, written at the end of so called christian time. Anno domini has past and Satan is reborn, the god/goddess of self; in the year of our lord and lady, man and woman. If you are a brother or sister of Satan, it is your duty to spread the teachings of this book and its connected attributes. Go and say I am mine own savior and scream that their christ is dead. Death to jesus, death to jesus, death to jesus, death to jesus, death to jesus, death to jesus, death to jesus, death to jesus, death to jesus, death to jesus, death to jesus, death to jesus, death to jesus!!!!!!

Part I The God Goddess of Self: Revised

Chapter 1 The Black Order

The Black Order has risen from the ashes of christian hypocrisy. Here me children of earth, the church of christ be vanquished! For here stands Satan's Church for all eyes to gaze upon and bare witness, to my testimony. I tell you, this is The Temple Of Life.

We stand for our Truth, Justice, Satanic Moral Freedom, and Love for all of our True Brothers and Sisters. Satan means The Spirit Of The Adversary, and is the legendary Adversary of the christian religion and god, adopted and transformed eclectically from many religions, mainly Greek, and Semitic/Egyptian beliefs. Satan represents ourselves as Gods and Goddesses, and our God/Goddess of Creation. Satan is our International/Global Concept, allying us against judeo-christian beliefs, laws, moral-values, and oppression. The Vampir Satanist 999 must commune and organize, establishing a new social/economic order, and will never repent or conform completely to a society that expels us and our opposing moral beliefs.

Man is God and God is Satan. Woman is Goddess and Goddess is Satan. Satan is the concept of Creation, Unity, and Self-Alliance. This is a new order of Man, Woman, Self-God, Self-Goddess, and Satan.

We accept Satan as a kind of National Concept, which is truly an International or Global Concept of Unity. This Concept is centered around anti-christian moral-values, which crystalizes the ideal concept of an Anti-Savior within our Church Of The Antichrist. We advocate all sexual freedom, racial harmony, and social/economic liberation, through a form of Spiritual Egalitarianism. We walk together under one banner, behold The Eye Of Satan! This is the Eye of Man, Woman, Self-God, Self-Goddess, and Creation.

We stand against any religion or organization that hinders our sexual freedom, our sensible moral and logical judgement, and our freedom to change the image and moral standards of mainstream or ruling society, toward a new, more realistic, sensible, universally beneficial, and advanced moral-value system. We also stand against any organization specifically designed to maintain and defend a small and limited percentage of people within an upper class economic state, while at the same time, maintaining and holding down/oppressing a much larger percentage of people within a lower class economic state. This type of class system uses the lower class as the work force, in a form of organized destitution slavery or poverty slavery.

We have entered the Age of High Technology and supposed moral liberation, yet we are still oppressed by judeo-christian dogma and rich class poverty slavery. How does such corruption and oppression exist in these times?

While religious leaders are squabbling over petty sexual moralities, and political officials are catering to their parties, religious supporters, and their corporate sponsors, the real problems are ignored, steadily growing worse. Why is it, that the rich grow fatter and we can see no end to the terror of international or global poverty slavery? It is a fact that the wealthy cannot survive without an underclass. Meaning, to rid the world of poverty slavery, would rid the world of the sovereignty of the rich class, through wealth limitations, and class submergence.

This kind of capitalist organization is designed to maintain a perpetual lower class, holding a majority of the world's people in a perpetual state of poverty. This is Poverty Slavery and it is Corrupt and a Crime to Humanity! Your children's, children's, children, will be born into this poverty slavery, unless they come from a rich bloodline, or we adopt a more advanced economic system.

While businesses leave the country to save money, and machines replace jobs, poverty slavery, and other crimes shall increase. While our school systems are in ruin, and lack the right security in a legal gun environment, more children will suffer from under education and lose their lives. While our economy goes further into recession, which will happen over and over because of this unbalanced system, who is going to suffer the most? Our Children! While government and homophobic military jobs decrease and corporate america skyrockets and you're powerless without a worthy union, you're going to suffer the hand of this form of capitalist corruption, poverty slavery!

When christian priests ask for donations, how does this help you? How does this affect your family? What kind of person is this that says praise jesus, and drives a mercedes benz? Christianity teaches you to believe in jesus, a pacifist. We all know that most christians are not pacifists, but major hypocrites. Pacifism, teaches you to willingly give in physically to your enemies, your oppressors. This would make me willingly powerless to stop my corrupt enemies/oppressors from enslaving and controlling my family and myself. Christianity is the pacifist's religion. Christianity is a perfect tool/weapon for the hypocrites to use to rule the world. So, let me see, I should be nonviolent and love mine enemies?

Vampir Satanism 999, teaches you to believe in yourself first, before placing any belief in something external from your own thoughts, ideas, principles, etc. The road to self-enlightenment is long and more traveled today, than ever before. We do not support blind devotion or faith. If you're going to believe in something, you must first believe in your-self, and be self-confident enough to decide for yourself if a certain set of principles, beliefs, etc., are for you and you alone. We love those that deserve our love, our True Brothers and Sisters. We openly hate our enemies, our oppressors, and those that deserve our hate. We are truly anti-christian, anti-judaist, anti-moslem, and stand against any other religion that supports, follows, believes in, or represents the judeo-christian moral-value system. The truth is, everyone needs an allying concept to bring us all together or against.

The judeo-christian god does not exist in our world, minds, etc. Our Concept of Satan, teaches us to believe in ourselves first. Then we can decide whether or not to accept the ideal concept of Satanic Creation as The Greater Deity, and ourselves as Lesser Deities, yet One with our Satanic Creation.

Christians claim, if you don't follow them by believing in their god and jesus, that you are a follower of Satan and live in Sin. They then denigrate, and degrade us, calling us names such as pagans, and heathens. To accept such degrading and twisted terminologies as the name of your religion is ignorant and gives to them further justification and public okay through social conformity, power, or authority to continue to degrade you in such a devious way. It is also not our goal to conform to them or change, because of their fear of us. They see us as evil beasts that sacrifice, murder, demonize, terrorize their neighborhoods, seek to undermine their way of life, and authority over others. The truth is, we are here to undermine their way of life and completely destroy their authority, freeing ourselves from their oppression, restoring our rights, so that they may never be stolen again, secured for all eternity. We are The Spirit Of The Adversary, allied against judeo-christian authoritarianism, not authoritarianism in general. We stand tall with our opposing moral-values and will make this The Highest Cause. We do not advocate random acts of violence or destruction against our enemies yet support your total self-defense from these dogmites. Let us stand together under a far less hypocritical banner and unifying concept. Satan is a concept that epitomizes their greatest enemy, what they fear the most. According to them, we are all Satanists and Sinners anyway. So, let us become their greatest nightmare, don't worry about what they think, it's not about what they think, it's about us! I say to you, place your ego in Satan and erect The Lord Of Darkness.

Chapter 2 The Machine of Satan

Satan has a dualistic nature and so has two economic faces, capitalist and socialist. Her Socialist side does not advocate capitalist gain against its own people. For when the people are capitalists, they stand against each other for personal gain. If all you care about is personal gain, then you do not care about your people and the goals of your people as a whole. This will make you a solitary capitalistic Satanist. The Socialist Satanists are known as True Group Practitioners.

Satan has a goal for his and her people. Satan stands and says, I am the New Order, I am the New Religion. So out with the old and in with the new. You the people are Satan, for you are the new. Satan is a concept, standing against the old. Do not think Satan is a lesser god or according to christianity, a fallen angel, now an evil devil. Believe that Satan is your Soul-Motivation and the concept of Supreme Unity. Let the name Satan be embedded in your life.

Satan is just a name, yet a name of ultimate power. For Satan was chosen to become the concept of the Anti-christ. Those who stand with me will drive the winds of beckon. Those who stand against me will feel my current sweep you away!

The True Group Practitioners believe in using capitalism as a gain against our technical, solitary, enemies, including the judeo-christian alliance. So, shall we capitalize off of those who are our enemies.
Satan has become the name of our Creation. For The Eye of Creation is The Eye of Satan. Satan is both male and female, both positive and negative. Satan is a divine being found within the One Soul or heart of men and women, which are the minds of men and women, our consciousness. The Soul or Consciousness does not truly exist, separate from the body or creation, for mind and body are One. There is One Great Consciousness, this is The Great Self of Creation, we have honorably named Satan. Therefore, we are also calling or giving name to your-self as a national/international allying concept, which is Satan. Satan is the name given to Self and all Creation, though it does not matter if you have a name. The only reason we have chosen Satan, is because we are Anti-christian, and the name represents Anti-christian beliefs, and we need an allied ego. Through time the Alliance will discard this Ego's Symbolic Name Head, yet it shall remain the same Self-Alliance.

Satanic Creation is its own opposite. These opposites will embody masculine and feminine aspects. They are attributed to positive and negative. These forces correspond to the Self and the Ego and are eternally battling for supremacy. Therefore, I anticipate the split in the Alliance and have only to blame the Ego.

If you are fighting only for power, you have only to lose power and regain your enslavery again. So I say, rise against me children, for you have only to break your backs in labor. For everything has a cycle, and my cycle will end just as quick as yours. To you my loyal followers let your Ego be with Satan and we shall stand together. For Satan is yourself and your-self with Satan is magnified, a thousand fold.

Do not fight for leadership, for we are all different gears in The Machine of Satan, so each of us will perform a different task. If you let your ego come directly to your-self instead of your Ego into the Self of Satan as a whole, you will drop a monkey wrench into the intricate mechanics of Satan and cause its ultimate fowl. For example, if two groups decide to go against each other for the reigns of power, you will divide the ultimate power by placing Ego into your-self, instead of placing it into Self as a Whole, or Whole Unit, as One!

For if you are an arm of Satan, be an arm and be mightier than all others. If you are a leg of Satan, be a leg of Satan and be more supportive than all others. If you are the head of Satan, be smarter than all others, for you are the Pride of Satan's Alliance.

So I repeat myself in assurance. For if you are an arm, you are not just an arm, you are the arm of Satan, and shall you be stronger than all others. If you are a leg, you are not just any leg, you are the leg of Satan, and shall you be the greatest support ever. If you are a head, you are not just any head, you are a head of Satan, and shall you be smarter than all that oppose you. For you are The Pride of Satan. So shall an arm wield fire, for all shall fear the masked "gorilla troops." So shall the head command the arm, the leg, and the body. For the body connects them all and is counsel to the head. (I had a dream of real masked Gorilla Troops.) ---Anthropoid Ape men, similar to those in the classic Planet of The Apes.

Chapter 3 A Glimpse At Our Future Economy

Satan doesn't care what color you are. Satan doesn't care what race you are. Satan doesn't care what sex you are. Satan doesn't care what sex you like. What Satan cares about is your happiness and your satisfaction. Christianity takes that away from you. They'll say to you, you have sinned, repent, repent. Then they'll say, go and confess. They'll tell you when you're young, you're gonna go to hell. What kind of people, fill a child's mind with guilt and fear?

Together we can fight the social standard of a christian morality. We have the right to have beautiful sex anytime and with anybody willing. We must fight the deliberate embedding of the concept of marriage in our minds. We must fight the deliberate embedding of the concept of holy stature or reputation in our minds. For marriage does not really matter, and it does not really matter how many people you have had sex with, as long as you're responsibly safe.

Once people worshiped many Gods and Goddesses and they lived free to their will. Judeo-christianity turned many of theses Gods and Goddesses into devils, demons, and the way of evil. I say back, back you christians, do not step on Our Will! Do not try and control us! We are free and will rise again, in The Name of Satan, your Adversary!

If you claim to be a communist and are rich, you are lying, for you truly are a capitalist. Many communists continue to say, we are free from capitalism, when they are living in poverty. I say you are still a slave, when you are bound by money. Communism can only truly exist, where there is No Money. So you say, how then will we be motivated? Do not be fooled into believing money is the only way to motivate.

I will now introduce you to Satan's Workers Union and our Nine Step Program, a motivational plan which will create equality among its order. Each step is a class of honor. The higher your class, the higher your honor and influence or in other words your power. Each higher class will have greater control and access to budgeted supplies. Your class will continue to graduate as you reach the required level of prerequisites, which is determined by the work you have done and the years you applied yourself to that said work. Once you achieve a proposed class Nine status, you become an Elder and may retire if you wish at the expense of the alliance. To become an Elder is the highest status you can possibly achieve and the most respected and honored title among all the systemized classes or the people.

No one is truly free in any society, for you are all bound by responsibility. So the capitalist believes he or she is free from enslavement, by owning their own land, house, and transportational vehicles, etc. This helps create inequality and slavery for the poor. For the poor are oppressed by the rich, bound by the money, they do not have. For many of the rich acquired their wealth dishonorably. If you are forced into a society, you are a captive of that society. If you are bound by money, you are caught by the limitations it presents to you, when you do not have it. The poor will always be powerless without money in a capitalist society. You can slave or work your whole life and still have nothing, no power, no honor, no respect, nothing in a capitalist society. Satan's Workers Union and our Nine Step Program will create organized and systemized equality and at the end of your work career, you will have power, honor, respect, which equals wealth,
which is the complete attainment of dignity.

Chapter 4 One Great Mind

Welcome children, into the Light of Satan. Satan is your only friend, for he and she is within you. You are Satan and Satan is you. Satan means Adversary, as you are your own Adversary. Every one of you makes up another part of Satan. Satan is Creation and you are part of Creation. So all of you make up Satan together and you make up Satan when you are alone and separate. If you are your own Adversary, you will always fight your-self. So on a more grand scale you will continue to fight your-self. For out there in this world, you will find your enemies. These enemies are the exact opposite of your-self. These people are the ones who condemn your beliefs. These people are the ones who condemn Satan and Your-Self.

There is no heaven or hell. There is no savior and no soul. There is only your-self, here and now. When you die, you will cease to exist as you know your-self to be. Life and death do not really exist, only in your mind. You are part of Creation, so you will always exist. Your mind is where you think and become aware of your consciousness.

You could say your consciousness is your soul, but don't forget of your comparison, for it is only a comparison. They say you have an individual immortal soul and I deny this, yet say you will always exist. For your consciousness is your mind and Self is the Heart of Mind. This is the truth, there is One Great Mind, One Great Self. So when you die, you will find your-self alive, never knowing death. For your consciousness fears unconsciousness out of knowing you will be unaware of your surroundings, hence unconsciousness. (This is my truth!)

The meaning of life is heightened awareness and in this heightened awareness, we know averagely, we cannot be aware outside our-selves and so we have death, a lowered awareness or unawareness. We know subconsciously that being unaware means you're wide open to attack and are at the mercy of your enemies. So all our fear is fear of the dark and what's lurking there in the shadows, waiting to prey on you.

Man the hunted; man the prey; man the fearful; man the victim; man the loser, or the lost soul, and the end. The only Heaven you will know is the temporary one you create here in this world or I should say, in this life or existence.

Go without fear Brothers and Sisters, for Hell is a child's dream, the nightmare of all things unknown. So you will find Heaven to be an escape, when you know there is no escape, only to face your fears, face the unknown!

There have been many different beliefs and religions of the past that have had the same concepts and resemblance as the Satanism I am presenting to you in this book. For now it's time to reunite these beliefs and label them all as The Neo-Satanism, The New Satanism. These beliefs have been forced into oblivion by most of the modern monotheistic religions. So like every cause in the beginning seems hopeless and labeled rebellious, whence becomes the underdog of the major social atmosphere and most always an enemy of the existing authority.

Satan the underdog will rise from his and her murky bowels and stake a renewed claim in the world of endless war. You can never separate man from his duality and so we find ourselves in an eternal philosophical stalemate. For this is the war between logic and morality, and practicality divides them in a void called no-mans-land.

Practicality is where reality sets in and idealism fades, and is replaced by materialism or realism. The reality of Satan is a Martial Society and the ideal is a pure martial society. The practicality of Satan is that there will never be a pure martial society and never will any society be pure and true to one belief or religion.

Therefore, the pure martial society will become the dreaded less than pure society that will rebel against it-self. So we conceive the almost pure martial society and the true satanic conformist which conforms to survive, and get ahead like all creatures of nature.

Chapter 5 Evil The Natural Mind

Evil is the natural mind that stalks and captures its prey. Good is the natural mind that sets free the victim, if not devoured when done. So shall the victim value their freedom and the victor, identified as The Master of The Game or Hunt. Outside the social statuses of humankind is nature's wild society. There you will find very few victims are set free and nature's evil prevails. Though, here in humanity's societies we are not immune to wild society. For it spills over upon us as we are constantly reminded that human societies are kingdoms within the Master Kingdom, The Wild Kingdom. So here too, we will find victims, upon victims, upon victims. For, man cannot escape the wild, as it is in him; in his blood; in his mind; in his being, or immortal soul. Man is evil and good.

The only good man is the man without victims of his folly. This man would be without food to eat, clothes to wear, friends to love or hate, all possessions, all sight, all sound, all thoughts, including body and mind. For, to be all good is not to be man, but pure force, divine force or god. This would be the god of light, though you cannot have light without darkness. This would be the goddess of darkness and so we see the duality that cannot be separated, and this is the same for man and woman. They say man is created in god's image, not the woman. God being a masculine force, which I am comparing to the good force in which judeo-christians interpreted it, is incomplete, as it is only half of it-self.

They have egotistically made or called their god a man or male exaltation, though we can perceive the equal forces of man and woman. The Goddess being a feminine force is what they have dogmatized as the devil or Satan. These two great forces combine into one beautiful God/Goddess of Self, in which we call Creation or Satan, because we are against christianities egotistical patriarchal philosophy.

A God/Goddess cannot be a God/Goddess without the knowledge and wisdom of eternal life and death. For, we shall attain this knowledge through our-selves. Eve is our Goddess Queen and Lilith is her lover, while Adam is their slave.

The Novice's Handbook
Of
Magick

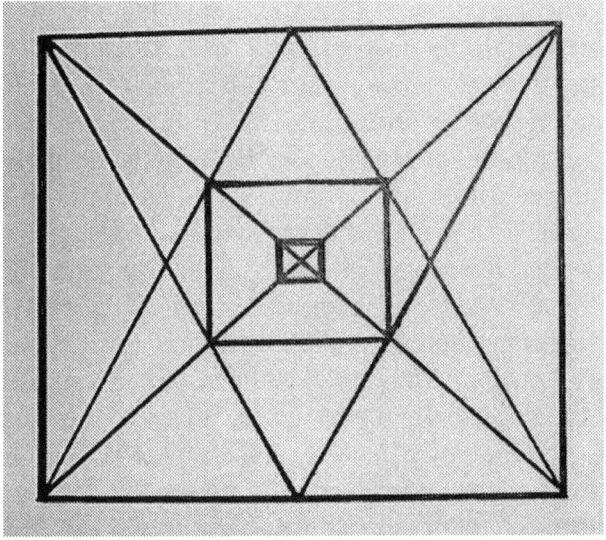

Introduction

I have a few different names for my Black Magick, cause names are important, but I'll talk about that later. This I will call Satanic Sorcery or Satanic/Vampiric Sorcery! This is the ancient unconventional art of mental and physical attainment. We all want to learn how to use this art for the purpose of attaining power in one form or another. If you don't seek power, then there is no reason for you to seek the knowledge of my art! We are dealing with different forces, which we will manipulate towards our will. First of all, we need a power base from which to construct our power vortex, from which each one of us will benefit. This is called the Temple! Then we need the Instrument of Power itself. In the old days, this was called the Magick Wand! I have transformed this instrument into my Bible! Black Magick, Satanic/Vampiric Sorcery, is 90% physical/material manipulation and 10% Mental/spiritual-fantasy imagery. By the way, my Spiritual Alchemy has the complete opposite formula. Therefore, this is realistically a very powerful art of mind control! The goal of which, is to mutually benefit each member of our Order. We are going to transform mental power/energy or knowledge into physical power/energy and the main physical tool/weapon of power in this society comes in a talismanic form called money. I will teach you about charms and talismans later; they are very important to our success. Let me give you a basic chart that we can use as a universal key, which most of you should know already, if you really have been studying magick in any school of thought. We will be using these two branches together, in the generation of power!

Basic Magickal Attributions Chart

Left	-Attribution-	Right
Physical		Mental
Non-emotional		Emotional
Realistic + Materialistic		Spiritualistic + Fantasy

A.   B.

Manipulation + Self-Control and Discipline   Ritual + Ceremony

1. Illusion
2. Transference
3. Interference
4. Charms / Talismans
5. Healing Arts
6. Martial Arts Procedure

1. Oath / Anugeration Baptismal c
2. Holy Day / Holiday / Sacred Day c
3. Chrm /Spell / Incantation / Song r
4. Divination r
5. Funeral / Wake / Last Rites c
6. Healing Arts with Ritual/Ceremonial Procedure
7. Martial Arts with Ritual/Ceremonial Procedure

Ceremonial Procedures

1. All ceremonial and ritualistic magick needs some sort of system to be based upon. I use a necromantic system including spirits of the dead, spirits of the living, negative forces or demonic forces, positive forces or angelic forces, gods, goddesses, creation, etc. These will be the forces which you will be summoning, and communicating your desires and will with and through.
2. All the intellectual preparation and purpose for the ceremony or ritual must be thought out, set up, and devised before hand. This is important because intellectualizing during the ceremony and ritual will disturb and break your emotional concentration and build up toward complete emotional release.
3. All ritual and ceremonial tools must be assembled. All ritual uniforms, clothing, robes, etc., must be ready or adorned. The ritual chamber must be fully prepared. The altar must be completely in order. The participants gathered. The purpose behind the ritual already known and everything pre-choreographed.
4. A list of the ceremonial tools to be used: Athame, Black Candle, Other Candles, Sword, Goblet or Chalice, Wine, Gong, Music, Bell, Incense, Incense Burner, Black Robes, Red Robes, Symbol of Baphomet or Unicursal Hexagram Medallions, or Ankhs, Skull, A Wall Emblem, Mats, etc.
5. Ritualistically purify the temple or ritual chamber room using incense and the incense burner. Make sure you clean the room first, removing dirt, dust, garbage, anything that can interfere with the flow of energy and degrades the purity of the ritual chamber. All tools must also be cleansed and purified as well as the altar.
6. This step is optional! The gong is rung once to begin a ritualistic group meditation on the purpose and goal of the ritual. Either appropriate music is played or the gong can be struck once a minute. After 10 minutes all must perform several yoga exercises guided by the head priest/ess or current celebrant. This will further focus the energy and help raise kundulini or chi.
7. All participants then take their places and the head priest/ess begins the ceremonial calls and the participants act out their parts in turn or all together. Once this has been completed then the celebrant begins to read the doctrine of the ceremony or the purpose. This will be accompanied by chants from the participants, music, etc. Also, you'll be using the tools

according to the ceremonial procedures. Finally, an emotional climax will be built up and a final release. Some ceremonies will be engaged in full ritualistic orgies at this time, which had followed the entire coven drinking of the ceremonial wine from the chalice.

8. At the complete end the gong or bell may be struck or sounded 3 times or 9 if better and another ritualistic cleansing and purification take place as the incense burner is waved from one end to the other. The candles blown out, etc.

Part VIII Satan's Hammer

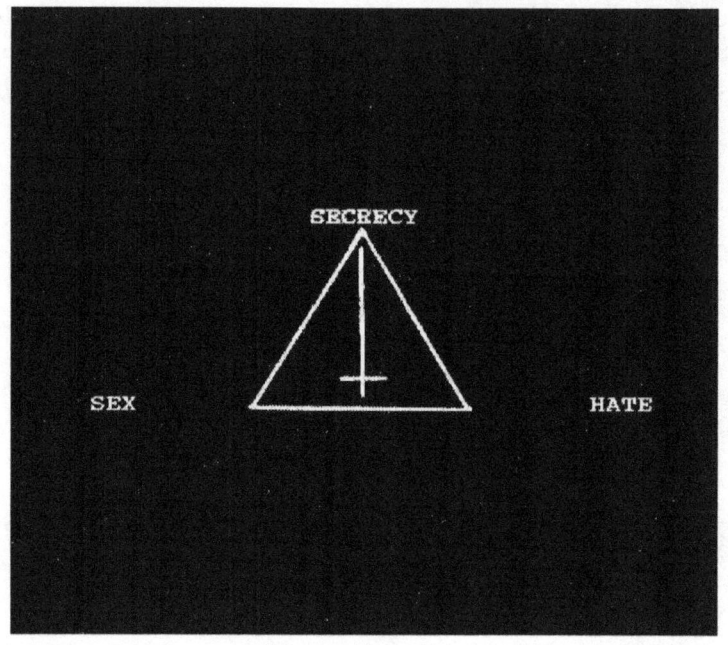

Part 1 Secrecy

Carry none, for they hold you down. Let the Church's secrets destroy them, internally. Satan has sent the Demon of secrecy into their lair. No one knows the power of this Demon. What does it truly represent? So as I said, no one knows the power of this Demon, for you would be dead!

Secrecy has been a logical way to survive and flourish. This ultimately means it is used against you. For Satan says, my first weapon against the Church is Secrecy, moreover a counter Secrecy. If you reveal everything, you shall have nothing to hide.
Through this you can not be exposed for attack. The Church itself is shrouded in Secrecy, from the top. When I say Church, I mean the roman catholic church. This is because you must destroy the heart of your enemy, to kill him. The catholic church is the core of all christendom and will be the center of our Master's attack. Satan orders all of us, his minions to uncover all of our secrets and be open about all things. For this will make you stronger in the light of Christian hypocrisy. Jesus never preached secrecy, only in a sense of doing things publicly, just to be praised. Secrecy is a sign of fear, maybe the Church is afraid of their own destruction. Do not fear the end, for it will come to all, somehow, as something new takes your place. To cover yourself in shrouds, will only make you blind to your own hypocrisy. For when you are made naked, you will run and hide yourself from the eyes of others, of God, of Satan. Then you will cover yourself with twice as many shrouds, as your lies deepen and spread your hypocrisy. Then it will touch your feet as well as your head and you will be soaked in death.

For your students will feel your hypocrisy and turn to me, the true revelation. I am the grand master, lowering the boom.

Part 2 Hate

Go and hate your enemies, for you shall not be without a shield. The Church hides its own hate from itself and so is deluded, dividing their loyalties, which makes them vulnerable in the face of the strong. Satan has sent the Demon of Hate into their lair.

Hate has been a logical way of dealing with your enemies. So you must know, it has been used against you, by all, christians, God, and Satan. For Satan says, "My second weapon against the Church is Hate." If you hate everyone, you will have no one to love. Through this you cannot be defenseless, against attack. The Church itself is derived from hate, an inverted hypocritical love that attacks all those who are different from what they believe. Satan demands that you hate all your enemies openly, instead of hypocritically, from behind a white washed cloak of illusion. Jesus never preached hate, but he hated his people for worshiping two gods hypocritically. "Give to Caesar, what is Caesar's, give to God, what is God's." The Church shall be crushed by its own hate, its own hypocrisy. Even jesus would say, "Remove the plank from your own eye, before you complain about the speck of sawdust in someone else's." So as the Church dissolves, they will turn against themselves, out of complete confusion. Satan declares, "We have won!" Sodom and Gomorrah have risen and Satan anoints his son, the true christ, The Great Anti-christ. I have come children, openly love your true Brothers and Sisters, and openly hate your true enemies.

Part 3 Sex

You are free to engage in all your sexual desires. The Church is bound by itself, tormenting itself day and night. So shall they fall through their own natural desires. Satan has sent the Demon of Lust into their lair.

Sex has been a logical means of satisfaction, ever since its discovery. Though it is a great source of enjoyment, it has been used against you, by all, by christians. For, it is a powerful charm at your disposal and only your idiocy and irresponsibility can allow it to harm you. For Satan says, "My third weapon against the Church is Sex." If you aren't free to your own sexual desires, you are a slave to someone else's beliefs. Satan commands you to be sexually free, this includes celibacy, if you choose. I tell you, jesus never preached against sex or for celibacy. Satan says, "Go and finally be free." The Beast of Celibacy will drive the celibate mad, going against his or her own natural desires. For your weakness, is only my power, calling you back to truth, to freedom, to desire. If your self calls you up, then go up above. If your self calls you down, then go down below.
If you find strength to overcome your weakness, then this was your true path and I'll set you free. Satan, the other face of God, is all giving in its ways. Evil was only the product of fear, a measurement of God.
The divine force gives and takes mysteriously, when you are ignorant of the truth. When you are all understanding and knowledgeable of the true truth, the mystery will become perfectly unraveled in the eyes of majesty, the living Gods and Goddesses. For I say, "The Church has fallen!"

Part IX Holy Days

The Great Saturnalia

"Saturday will be our day of joy and merriment!"

The Great Saturnalia, The Feast of Saturn has been chosen by The First Priest as our Sacred Festival. This is in correlation with the completion of his Holy Book, Satan's Divine Vampire Bible! This festival will last a week or two, beginning on the eve of the holiday! For on the 15, He had a vision of the hypocrisy of the world's religions. On the 16, of December 1999, The Holy Day of Pleasure began. This day of course will not end for a week or two. On this day, He had a revelation of the world's religions great demise! For in His Revelation was the completion of The Great Work! Each of our Brothers and Sisters will take The Sacred Sip, of The Sacred Wine, in remembrance and celebration of Our Triumph! There is the great and small, in all things! Therefore, we shall celebrate every Saturday, hereafter, remembering our Goddess/God, Ourselves, and Our Great Holiday, Our Holy Day of Pleasure! This will be our Night of The Sabbath! The lesser Sabbath will be a continuous event, hosted by our Brothers and Sisters! This event will only be open to members and initiates! Come join our celebration, Brothers and Sisters! For this is The Temple of Life!!!!!!

Part X The Great House of Polygamy

Introduction

Polygamy is the advanced and beautiful lifestyle of having more than one bride or groom(polyandry). It is founded upon the belief and practice of polyamory, the ability and willingness to love more than one other person, etc., at one time or the same time. It is also founded upon the desire and willingness to engage in promiscuous sex with as many partners as we choose and when we choose, without discrimination or condemnation from inferior, idealistic, fanatical, and basically unnatural judeo-christian moral-values.

We publicly declare the right to defy judeo-christian dogma and civil laws, loving and wedding who we desire to and will to love and wed, when we wish to do so.

Our New Age Lifestyle is not exactly new it has been practiced by many ancient cultures, before the advent of judeo-christian monogamous fanaticism or fascism. There were many cultures that enjoyed monogamy, but they never condemned polygamy in the least.

Monogamy and Polygamy (polyandry) existed alongside each other happily, until the rise of such fanaticism/fascism. It is only those religions that don the judeo-christian banner and seek to institutionalize the dogmatic judeo-christian moral-value system that condemns polygamy.

Our goal is to rise to a higher more loving relationship, escaping greed, possession, jealousy, cheating, lies, fighting, and hating those you truly love. We seek to raise the status of maturity within the culture through moving beyond such inferior qualities, which we continue to pass on to our children. We intend to teach our children the superiorly divine beauty of sexuality, polyamory, and polygamy. Our future will not be filled with stagnate, oppressive beliefs out of the dark ages of human history. Our future will be filled with great beauty, joy, pleasure, and fulfillment beyond human imagination. We will send these useless, oppressive, false religions back to the darkest pits from which they've come. This is The Age of Fire! This is The Age of Humanity! This is The Age of The Great House of Polygamy!

Pre-Nuptials And Benefits

All family members that officially break ties with or divorce from the family, leave with what wealth they joined with, minus contributions to the family wealth or treasury. All members maintain separate treasuries at their will or according to the capability, based upon the type of economic system. All members enter into a Pre-Nuptial Agreement, which clarifies that all parties leave with what they joined with, minus contributions and personal choice expenses. The only ones that must receive benefits are children, and this comes out of the family treasury. These benefits don't have to be monetary.

The Individual

The individual is someone outside of all family houses that really has no title or power, within any House of Polygamy. They remain so until they wed into a family, wedding a Master or Mistress, or they apply for Master or Mistress Status. The individual and their children cannot receive benefits from the family treasury, only the Master or Mistresses personal treasury.

The Master or Mistress

Anyone who is a member of our church may apply for an Official Master or Mistress Title, which empowers you as the Master of your New House. The Master or Mistress is responsible for overseeing the House or Family Treasury and setting up most family regulations, such as contributions, work, benefits, etc. The Master may wed other Masters or Mistresses, combining their family treasury. If they divorce, family treasury is always divided according to what they wedded with, based upon Pre-Nuptial Agreement, minus losses, contributions, benefits, etc. A House of many Masters and Mistresses may appoint Lords or Ladies from among their family circle of Masters and Mistresses to oversee different functions and aspects of the family, and family business.

The Concubine

The Concubine is anyone without title, general family, or anyone who steps down from Master or Mistress, and Weds a Master or Mistress. The number of concubines or wives/grooms a Master or Mistress may have is unlimited. They have no major responsibilities overseeing family affairs and business.

General Family

General family includes children, teens, and anyone who remains in the family and does not apply for Master or Mistress Status.

The Royal Master Or Royal Mistress

This is an In-House Status and they have no power over the affairs of the House they were born into, unless appointed by the overseers or if the overseers became completely inactive and or incapable of fulfilling their responsibilities on an average day to day basis.

Part XI Advanced Principles

The Principles
Of
The Anti-christ Religion

1. **Anti-circumcision/Anti-baptism:** We are against circumcision! Circumcision is a sign of the jew and christian covenant to their god. This is a primitive practice which destroys the natural external beauty of the human body. We hold no covenant with the jew/christian god, only ourselves and creation. We are anti-baptism as well. Baptism represents the christian initiation ritual upon entering their church. This ritual is usually performed shortly after birth, to begin the child's inculcation and indoctrination as soon as possible. We abhor this practice and believe that any form of initiation must take place when a human is of a mature age of understanding, education, experience, and wisdom.

2. **Anti-monotheism:** We support polytheism, pantheism, and atheism. Having or holding more than one god or belief and respecting other deities/beliefs in mutual respect is superior to monotheism. Polytheism/Pantheism is the key to unity and everlasting harmony! –Pantheism should be known as the Creationism and what is known as the christian creationism should be called zionist science.

3. **Anti-spirit worship:** We support physical/material human body worship. We worship the beauty and pleasure of the human body! The human body is the highest and most important aspect of our existence and the ultimate object of our will and desires. We believe in worshipping the human body as an object of carnal reverence and sexual delight. The sacred carnal flesh is blessed with sacred sexuality!

4. Anti-monogamy/Anti-marriage: We support polyamory, promiscuousness, polygamy, bigamy, polyandry, and misogamy. We support polygamy and stand for Anti-monogamy, and Anti-virgin purity. We support and teach Anti-marriage/misogamy or teach polygamy. We do not teach monogamy, but it is up to each individual to choose their lifestyle.

5. Anti-heterosexuality: We support homosexuality and bisexuality. We are Anti-heterosexual when it comes to the mainstream of society. Through teaching and spreading heterosexuality, homophobia and anti-gay beliefs are spread as well. Through that homophobic culture gays and bisexuals face extreme condemnation and discrimination. By teaching against total heterosexual lifestyles, we eliminate the majority of homophobic and anti-gays beliefs and fears. This is not a stand against heterosexuality in general, meaning it will not arise as hatred toward heterosexuals, because we teach and promote bisexuality. Heterosexuality becomes more than common place and typical among lifestyles that also embrace the same sex. The total heterosexual will be rare and a minority, that will face little condemnation. We teach that we are born in a natural and beautiful bisexual or androgynous state. We therefore teach against a mainstream heterosexuality through a form of Anti-heterosexuality, though it is up to each individual to choose their lifestyle.

6. Anti-homogenization: We support religious, political, economic, and racial, etc., segregation on a higher level to ensure equality and respect the rights of those who believe in their type of environment. Mutual Segregation is superior to homogenization, which is designed to limit, control, and empower only one specific belief system, or political/economic system. This means that those who wish to live in a homogenized state may do so and those that do not are free to segregate into their own unified state or power.

Laws of Organizational Integrity

1. To defeat oppressive opponent religions you must secure power over them. Without power over them, they will forever advance upon you with beliefs, laws, guns, economically, etc., oppressing you with natural dominance. Through securing power over them the tables are turned.

2. Anti-religion does not secure power over oppressive opponent religions. This is because there will never be a world where the majority of people are Anti-religion or Anti-belief based. There will always be a dominant foundational core moral-value system.

3. Organized oppositional adversarial belief systems and religions secure power over opponent religions. True and Great Organizations are developed through allegiance and dedication to a Master Belief System and its ultimate goals. Great Organization alone is power over your opponents and a blockade to their progress.

4. The Constructive Unity and Conformity of your oppositional adverarial belief systems and religions secure power over opponent religions. Unity is synonymous with Conformity, when you stand before an opponent a thousand times your strength. The Individual Intelligence is Great but it is no match for the Gnashing of the jaws of the Multi-headed, Multi-intelligent Hydra. Alone you will be ripped to shredded pieces on the battlefield of Life and Existence.

5. Resistance to the organization must be eliminated within the inner ranks and those that pose a threat to the security of the order must be outcast. Inner turmoil and dispute creates violent waves of destruction to the Social Skeleton of your

Organization. The Social Skeleton must be at harmony with it's branches. If they resist, remove them from the center and place them near the outer reaches where they can do little harm stirring up a social calamity. Those that are a security risk must be watched and examined, while kept far from your war rooms and secret meetings. Denigration may be employed toward the resistance factions as a military tactic keeping out the unwanted and keeping those who want to stay from thinking they can get away with the same behavior. Also, denigration may help to weaken the minds of the resistance factions.

6. Those dedicated and loyal to the organization must do some work to help advance the organization and build up its financial and substance based power structures. Organization Members can't just sit by idlly and not take part in any of the work that the Organization is working toward. It is so important that the Members show their allegiance by taking part in one form or another, which will impact beneficially on the Order. This is True Loyalty, and anything less is Disloyalty and another sign of artificial conviction, and passive resistance.

Part XII The New Sciences

The Laws of The New Social Sexual Psychology

1. Sex is a Need, not just a desire. Humans need to be sexually fulfilled, in order to escape sexual repression and attain maximum morale. The lack of sexual fulfillment, will lead to sexual repression, causing natural depression, anxiety, melancholy, collapse of self-esteem, collapse of self-confidence, etc. These natural personality traits or characters, can lead to more natural, yet external reactions that may harm the individual or others. These characters can manifest as suicidal tendencies, homicidal tendencies, and sexual assault or rape, etc.

2. Love is a Need, even if it is but a chemical emotion. The individual needs to be loved by another person or more, and also needs to love another person or more, to maintain an average mental state of health, which is based upon a degree of selfesteem, self-confidence, degree of motivation to accomplish some task or purpose, and a degree of social sexual libido, etc.

3. All Emotions, Feelings, Actions, and Reactions are Normal. There is no such concept of abnormality, or insanity, especially when dealing with the mind. There is not one thought, belief, or action that is abnormal. All attempts to abnormalize a feeling, action, or belief, is characterized by the influence of ones own moral beliefs and therefore it is a contamination of thought and diagnosis. This natural tendency to introduce ones own moral into the examination of another beings world, is part of our survival instincts, set on primeval domination. There is no way, to completely rid ourselves of such thought, because these separate Laws of Animal Dominion can not be escaped, no matter how hard we try to ascend into our ideal spiritual nature.

This in general means that, depression, suicide, war, rape, murder, pedophilia, etc., are all natural actions, based upon natural desires, emotions, and feelings. We must remember, we are not the judges of moral action, but the healers of natural symptoms. The old psychologists and psychiatrists became the guardian institutes sponsored by the governments and drug companies, to maintain and control those individuals that were mainly less criminal, and disrupted the flow of mainstream or the majority of society, with its dominant institutionalized moral-value system. Once again, this is a reflection of our Primeval Natures and the Laws of Animal Dominion. Since we too are forced into this position, we must endeavor to make sure that the dominant social sexual moral-value system is just, and free from fanaticism, since we have been placed in the position of judge and jury of the lesser gods and goddesses, The Super-Human Beings.

The Primeval Laws Of Animal Dominion

There are four principle primeval laws of animal nature that will always exist. These laws concern all of animal dominion, but the study of our science is more directly concerned with all human social, cultural, economic, political, religious, and military societies or civilization, etc. No matter how civilized you claim to be or how religiously, spiritually, and morally fanatical you become, because of your ideal fantasies or programs, these laws shall rule over you.

Everyone who claims that violence and hatred are primitive actions and emotions, is trying to or is enforcing their moral opinions, through these very same laws that in essence are of your nature. The question is not who is right or wrong. The question becomes, who is trying to dominate, using whatever belief as a tool or weapon to dominate? Most might never realize this, until it is pointed out to them. The belief itself has power and used like a sword, harnesses more power, drawing in the like minded, which then reinforces their dominion, spreading it out further. We will gather together, based upon these laws of dominion, which dictates our universe. These laws transcend all human advancement, but can be used to benefit humanity.

According to our scientific laws, two great forces will always rise above the rest, and one will always dominate the other. We will eternally struggle to attain domination, escaping domination, or struggle to maintain our domination, fighting off being dominated.

First, you must understand what you believe and through this, whose side do you stand upon? There is no in-between, no neutrality, for in the end, there will only be two sides. Second, you must decide truly, whether you wish to be a leader or a non-leader.

The leaders will be educated members of an elite core that will carry the weight of responsibility, through all decision-making positions.

The non-leaders will engage in the act of receiving and fulfilling the precise and delicately calculated decisions passed down to them.

Third, you must invest in your beliefs, if you truly believe in them. This can be done through physical work, mental work, or economic, and monetary support, etc.

Here are the four principle laws that dominate our lives:

1. Dominate or be dominated.
2. Strength in numbers.
3. New and better knowledge prevails over old and useless knowledge.
4. Order controls chaos.

Part XIII Temple of Kama

Tantric Hindu Beliefs

Dharma, Ahimsa, Artha, Kama, and Yoga are the five main methods of spiritual enlightenment which all complement each other and represent proper ways of living. This would be according to the interpretations set forth here. I consider myself a Tantric Hindu. We use all the Hindu Scriptures, as well as others, and the Hindu Pantheon of Deities, to help us understand our lives and the universe. This gives us a sense of our purpose here and why and how we should live a spiritual life.

Ahimsa

Ahimsa is one of the main spiritual focuses of our Temple of Kama. Ahimsa means non-injury or nonviolence and a deep spiritual ideal of not harming other life forms. There are degrees of Ahimsa which we may try to respect when dealing with the practicality of situations. At all times we try to live a nonviolent existence which will help to eliminate karma and bring about a peaceful world in which to live and prosper spiritually. This happens by teaching Ahimsa along with our other ideals to help us achieve enlightenment through a spiritual health consciousness.

Dharma

Dharma is another one of our focuses. It represents divine truth, balance, and law. Here devotees are bound to the Dharma of our moral-value system, and other doctrines. Dharma can be said to be righteous living and we dedicate our lives to the Dharma. Dharma can also be associated with the idea of a judgment and the divine truth or life-force that fills the entire universe or Creation and is within every single one of us. We seek out the Dharma throughout our entire lives and it guides us to a state of liberation, freedom, or Moksha through our spiritual health consciousness.

Moksha

Moksha is liberation or freedom, much like nirvana or Samadhi. Though it is supposed to be liberation from the cycle of samsara or reincarnation and the end of suffering. This is only to be achieved through the Dharma or right living which includes the values set forth as the Dharma, Ahimsa, Kama, and Artha as set forth in our beliefs here. To practice Ahimsa, Kama, Dharma, and Artha properly as set forth here each involves sacrifice of the ego into the inner Self and Creation.

Karma

Karma is the idea of negative energies built up from negative actions and thoughts. These supposedly come back to us in out next lives. The idea is to live righteously and do good things for others and have good thoughts to eliminate Karma or negative Karma. Through this we escape the cycle of Samsara or reincarnation and achieve liberation Moksha. Karma is normally based upon the idea that each person has an individual soul and I believe that there is one great consciousness and so only one great soul. And each of us has to eliminate our Karma as one being to bring about a better world and to free those who seek freedom from the cycle of reincarnation which becomes a non-consecutive form of reincarnation in my system. The liberation is from the suffering but not life itself or Creation. And we have a choice to attain to living god-hood or eternal bliss. This can only be achieved through ego denial and unity dedicated to the spiritual health consciousness.

Non-Consecutive Reincarnation

Non-Consecutive Reincarnation is based upon the idea of a universal soul or life-force. We are but merely individual aspects of this great consciousness. We shall always exist and are reborn a thousand times before we ever die. This is like a great hydra with many heads and one dies. The creature does not die it only grows another head or many heads. Also, it's like a great ocean or lake. Out of the lake arises a life form and it lives its whole life and then returns to the lake and in an instant disburses into infinite particles that can never be traced and at all times new life forms are constantly emerging from the lake and returning.

Samsara

Samsara is the cycle of reincarnation which we go through until we eliminate Karmas and achieve Moksha. Though in my system we do not ever escape this cycle we only escape the suffering and live forever if we choose or we choose to embrace Nirvana or Moksha.

Spiritual Artha

Artha is known as prosperity and material wealth, though I see it as Spiritual and Material Wealth for all people in a state of super-equality brought about by the surrender of the ego to the inner-Self and Creation. Through this process all can attain to true prosperity together and live a very fulfilling life through the Temple and the Dharma of their Temple. Think of your Brothers and Sisters before your-Self. And Spiritual Wealth before Material Wealth. Those that seek only material wealth for themselves are unspiritual and this goes against our spiritual health consciousness. It is seen that those who perpetuate a monetary system that create classes or those that created castes that then creates a monetary system do so only to maintain control and power through their own ego fulfillment and do not practice Spiritual Ahimsa and fall short of practicing the Dharma. They will have the greatest Karmas that hold all of humanity back as a whole being.

Sacred Kama

Kama is the idea of sensual and sexual fulfillment and spiritual enlightenment through Tantric Rituals. Kama means Sacred Love or Sacred Sex. Through union of the masculine and feminine aspects of Creation, or a God and Goddess all of Creation was brought into existence and expanded into the material universe. And so since humans are part of Creation they are divine deities as well which reflect the Creation and so through their ritual reenactment of Creation's Copulation they raise Kundulini and achieve divine spiritual consciousness or divine spiritual health consciousness and also the sensual fulfillments all creatures need to become and remain healthy. And the symbols of sexuality are divine symbols such as the phallus and vulva or the lingam and the yoni. And the human body is the most sacred temple of all. Through this consciousness raising we bring about universal spiritual health consciousness and so the sacredness of Tantrism is established. All supporters should practice Kama to achieve the Dharma, Ahimsa, proper Karma, Artha, and Moksha.

Yoga Enlightenment

Yoga is the path of physical and spiritual enlightenment and healthy living. There are said to be hundreds of forms of Yoga but 8 limbs or branches. Most are familiar with Hatha Yoga with its positions. Meditation Yoga and Tantric Yoga are a few that we teach in our Temple. The Priest or Priestess practices Dharma which teaches us to be spiritually and physically healthy and it is the job of the Priests and Priestesses to learn various healing arts and heal others and teach others.

Part XIV The Nine Satanic Statements

The Nine Satanic Statements

1. There is no true Satanism, only your Satanism. One dogma begets another. A single person or group can never claim a monopoly on any religion. Here you will find Satanism 999.

2. The Satanist seeks out those like themselves to form a constructive and interdependent union which is the foundation of positive and constructive conformity. Those who seek pure independence should do so and find themselves outside of our group and enemies of the greater cause. Alliances with other groups are encouraged as long as the beliefs and goals are not completely oppositional.

3. The Satanist believes in a deity of creation, a deity within themselves, or both. What has religion become when you have completely removed the spirituality, mysticism, and sacred aspects from its foundation? Religion collapses into an ugly creature that has no breath of life and can only simply be called a philosophy. This if it can be called religion, is a dead religion. Without a deity of some sort to centralize your focus and creative wills, the need for that religion becomes futile and all worship degenerates into self gain and defilement of the sacred. The beauty of religion is in its grand architecture built upon a foundation of faith in some unknowable force rising up into its pillars of ecstasy. Blind devotion is only blind devotion when you are not allowed to ask why and question your faith or allegiance in some unknown entity or force.

4. The Satanist has individual personality and character but does not seek total independence from the group unless they have chosen to be their own group. As their own group they become an enemy of the greater group and may not be

respected or allied with depending upon how oppositional they have become.

5. The Satanist recruits as many other Satanists as possible. Strength in numbers always prevails and quality always rises anyway. Those that oppose open recruitment reveal their hypocrisy and are of their own group and an enemy to the greater cause.

6. The Satanist accepts the anti-christian or Satanic Moral-Value System in order to create balance where chaos has lurked in a vacuum of emptiness created by the elimination of the judeo-christian value-system. Where there is chaos order must always rise. Anarchy is an illusion that never lasts long.

7. The Satanist must always be loyal to their personal Temple or Church. If they are not loyal to one outside they will be loyal to one within. Disloyalty of any kind is forbidden and represents the work of the enemy. First a Satanist must find loyalty within, and then can choose a Temple outside them-self. All are born in the light of the disloyal minion and find the light of the loyal god/goddess of creation that we call Satan within or without.

8. The Satanist is the Super-Man and Super-Woman rising in absolute dominance against their opposition as an allied Super-Race within one body or structure known as The Alpha Force. Those that separate from The Alpha Force will feel its current, its power bearing down on them as individuals they will be no match for The Alpha Force. This is the path of superior attainment within the Super-Collective reflected in the Super-Self as godhood and goddess-hood.

9. The Satanist seeks out the most advanced knowledge, skills, arts, beliefs, sciences, and spirituality to become a complete universal being. The Satanist uses this knowledge to advance the whole Super-Collective. Old and useless knowledge is archived and burned away spiritually as the new is ritually accepted and used to advance our cause to attain mastery of ourselves and our universe. As ants in a giant's world, the giants step upon the ants until the ants collectively overpower the giants by covering his whole body. Then the giant will recognize our power, accept our Alpha Force, giving us our rights, free reign, etc., and either work with us or be destroyed.

Part XV The Antisaints

Introduction

I'd like to announce the resurrection and canonization of two Great Leaders and Founders of Modern Satanism. Each Founding Father possesses their own attributes and specialized contributions to the evolution of Satanism towards the birth of Vampir Satanism 999, through the marriage of aspects of both their religious philosophies, along with other eclectic visions. All humans have negative qualities and thus benefits that distort the path that we've chosen. Therefore, we seek to purge our founding fathers of these negative attributes and glorify them for what great accomplishments that they have achieved, which benefits the advancement of Satanism today and forevermore, especially within the new religion of Vampir Satanism 999.

First Antisaint

Our First Founding Father brought us a great deal of spiritual insight, scientific occult knowledge, and also taught us to accept the carnal as well. Many of you know him already as The Great Beast and his name will live in infamy in The Great Hall of Honor, Fame, and Glory. He is our Father Aleister Crowley and He is Thrice Great.
The following scriptures are the beginning of The Book Of Thelema/The Book Of The Law. It was dictated to The Now Ascended Master Aleister Crowley, through a kind of guardian and guiding spirit of great intelligence called Aiwass.

1. Had ! The Manifestation of Nuit.
2. The unveiling of the company of heaven.
3. Every man and every woman is a star.
4. Every number is infinite ; there is no difference.
5. Help me, o warrior lord of Thebes, in my unveiling before the Children of men !
6. Be thou Hadit, my secret centre, my heart & my tongue !
7. Behold ! it is revealed by Aiwass the minister of Hoor-paar-kraat.
8. The Khabs is in the Khu, not the Khu in the Khabs.
9. Worship then the Khabs, and behold my light shed over you !
10. Let my servants be few & secret : they shall rule the many & the known.
11. These are fools that men adore ; both their Gods & their men are fools.
12. Come forth, o children, under the stars, & take your fill of love !
13. I am above you and in you. My ecstasy is in yours. My joy is to see your joy.

14. Above, the gemmed Azure is
The naked splendour of Nuit ;
She bends in ecstasy to kiss
The secret ardours of Hadit.
The winged globe, the starry blue,
Are mine, O Ankh-af-na-khonsu !
15. Now ye shall know that the chosen priest & apostle of infinite space is the prince-priest the Beast ; and in his woman called the Scarlet Woman is all power given. They shall gather my children into their fold : they shall bring the glory of the stars into the hearts of men.
16. For he is ever a sun, and she a moon. But to him is the winged secret flame, and to her the stooping starlight.

Second Antisaint

Our Second Founding Father brought us a purely earthly and material outlook on life, completely grounded in the carnality of human existence. His realistic approach has drowned the spiritual, spawning and attracting many atheists internationally, which may serve our cause yet.
Though his greatest accomplishment was made through his inspiration from the dark force of nature, which was to invoke and spread The Great Name of Satan to multitudes of modern devotees and supporters of the cause. For this great deed alone he must be honored as we condemn his willful philosophy of the mercenary and spit upon lavey the animal and resurrect and Hail LaVey the chosen one. Many of you know him already as The Black Pope and his name will live in infamy in The Great Hall of Honor, Fame, and Glory. He is our Father Anton LaVey and He is Thrice Great.
Here are a few excerpts from LaVey's Satanic Bible. As far as I know, these were written by him, unlike much of his bible.
" When all religious faith in lies has waned, it is because man has become closer to himself, and farther from "God"; closer to the "Devil." If this is what the devil represents, and a man lives in the devil's fane, with the sinews of Satan moving in his flesh, then he either escapes from the cacklings and carpings of the righteous, or stands proudly in his secret places of the earth and manipulates the folly-ridden masses through his own Satanic might, until that day when he may come forth in splendour proclaiming, "I AM A SATANIST!,
BOW DOWN, FOR I AM THE HIGHEST EMBODIMENT OF HUMAN LIFE!" "

---NOW COMING FORTH PROCLAIMING I AM SATAN! I AM GOD!

" A group ritual is certainly much more of a reinforcement of faith, and an instillation of power, than is a private ceremony. The massing together of persons who are dedicated to a common philosophy is bound to insure a renewal of confidence in the power of magic. The pageantry of religion is what has sustained it. When religion consistently becomes a solitary situation it reaches into that realm of self-denial which runs concurrent with anti-social behavior. It is for this reason that the Satanist should attempt to seek out others with whom to engage in these ceremonies. "

Web Sites

http://thesatanicbibleshop.net
http://satansmodels.net
http://churchoftheantichrist999.net
http://templeofkama.net
http://templeofkama.com
http://caesarsindiashop.net

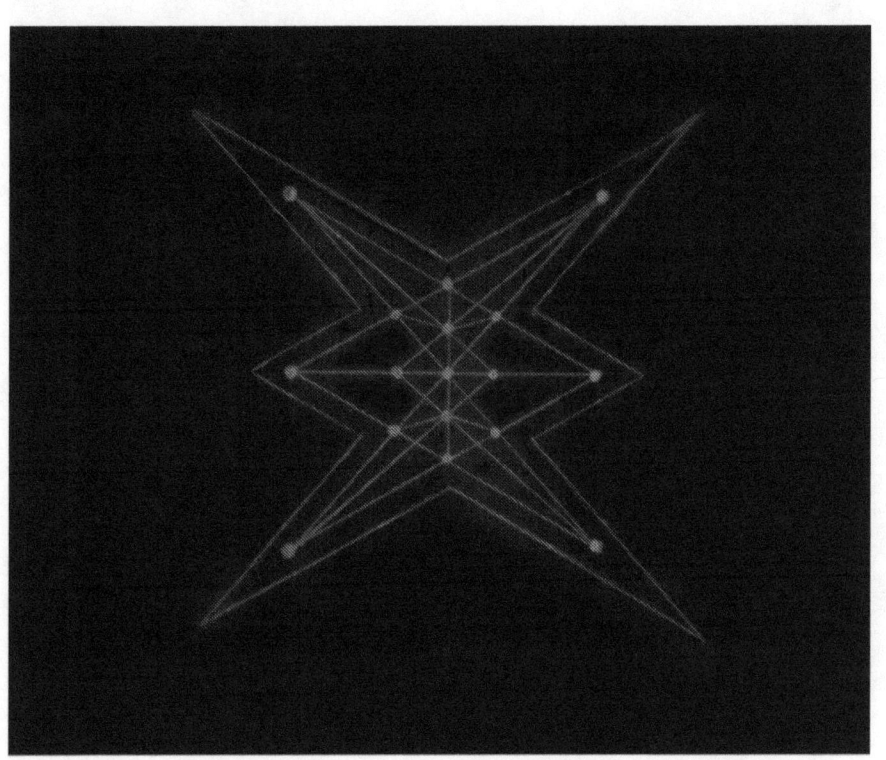

www.ingramcontent.com/pod-product-compliance
Lightning Source LLC
Chambersburg PA
CBHW021359290426
44108CB00010B/310